Eva Werner

Besser in

Englisch

8. Klasse
Gymnasium

Über die Autorin:
Eva Werner unterrichtet Englisch an einem Gymnasium.

Bildquellen:
Fotos privat

Bibliografische Information der Deutschen Nationalbibliothek
Die Deutsche Nationalbibliothek verzeichnet diese Publikation in der
Deutschen Nationalbibliografie; detaillierte bibliografische Daten sind im
Internet über http://dnb.dnb.de abrufbar.

Das Wort **Cornelsen** ist für den Cornelsen Verlag GmbH als Marke geschützt.

Kein Teil dieses Werkes darf ohne schriftliche Einwilligung des Verlages in
irgendeiner Form (Fotokopie, Mikrofilm oder ein anderes Verfahren), auch nicht für
Zwecke der Unterrichtsgestaltung, reproduziert oder unter Verwendung
elektronischer Systeme verarbeitet, vervielfältigt oder verbreitet werden.

Alle Rechte vorbehalten.
Nachdruck, auch auszugsweise nicht gestattet.

Für die Inhalte der im Buch genannten Internetlinks, deren Verknüpfungen
zu anderen Internetangeboten und Änderungen der Internetadressen kann der Verlag
keine Verantwortung übernehmen und macht sich diese Inhalte nicht zu eigen.
Ein Anspruch auf Nennung besteht nicht.

2. Auflage
© Cornelsen Scriptor 2012   D   C   B
Bibliographisches Institut GmbH
Mecklenburgische Straße 53, 14197 Berlin

Redaktionelle Leitung: Constanze Schöder
Redaktion: lüra – Klemt & Mues GbR
Illustrationen: Dorina Teßmann
Herstellung: Annette Scheerer
Layoutkonzept: Horst Bachmann, Weinheim
Umschlaggestaltung: glas AG, Seeheim-Jugenheim
Satz/Layout: Carola Fuchs, Berlin
Druck und Bindung: AZ Druck und Datentechnik GmbH,
Heisinger Straße 16, 87437 Kempten
Printed in Germany

ISBN 978-3-411-87079-0

Inhaltsverzeichnis

Vorwort 5

1 Revision 6
Conditional clauses – Bedingungssätze 6
Active or passive voice? 8
Future perfect 9
Past perfect 10
Reported speech 11
Relative pronouns and contact clauses 13

2 Sprache verstehen 14
   2.1 *The gerund* 14
   2.2 *Gerund and/or infinitive?* 16
   2.3 *Reported speech* 18
   2.4 *The present perfect progressive* 23
   2.5 *Relative clauses* 26
   2.6 *Definite/indefinite article* 29
   2.7 *Mediation* 31
   Test 31

3 Texte verstehen 44
   3.1 Lesen und verstehen 44
      Fictional texts 44
      The last Native American's dream 45
      Prefixes and suffixes 49
      Intelligent guessing: new words 50
      The Tanaeka ritual 51
      British English – American English: spelling 57
      British English – American English: vocabulary 58
      Factual texts from newspapers or the Internet 60
      Drugs gain victory over rural areas 61
      How to write a summary 64
      Emphasis with -self and do/did 65
   Test 68

Inhaltsverzeichnis

	3.2	Hören und verstehen	72
		Milestones in American History: the Boston Tea Party	74
		Uscful vocabulary	74
		British and American pronunciation	78
		Teenage life in Britain and the USA	79
		Stop: Mistake!	80
	Test		82
4	**Texte schreiben**		86
	4.1	Mit vorgegebenen Informationen Texte erstellen	86
		Guided writing	86
		Before writing the text	88
		Improving your text	89
	4.2	Eine Reisebroschüre erstellen	93
	4.3	Briefe verfassen	95
	4.4	Geschichten zu Bildern schreiben	100
		Free text composition	100
		Checklist: How to write your text	103
		Arbeit mit einem einsprachigen Wörterbuch	105
		Free text composition	100
	4.5	Zeitungsartikel schreiben	106
		Different kinds of newspaper	108
	Test		110

Stichwortverzeichnis   112

Vorwort

Liebe Schülerin, lieber Schüler,

du hast hier ein Buch zum Lernen, Wiederholen und Üben in der Hand.
- ▷ Die Themen sind in kleinen, verständlichen Schritten aufbereitet.
- ▷ Schaffe dir parallel zu diesem Buch ein Arbeitsheft an, in das du hineinschreiben kannst.
- ▷ Ein Lösungsheft hilft dir, deine Ergebnisse zu kontrollieren.
- ▷ Mit der beiliegenden CD und vielen Übungen dazu kannst du dein Hörverstehen trainieren. Folgender Hinweis zeigt dir, wo du die CD verwenden musst: **Track**

Mit diesem Buch kannst du auf zweierlei Weise arbeiten:

1. Möglichkeit:
Wenn du dich im Fach Englisch insgesamt ein wenig unsicher fühlst, solltest du das Buch von vorn bis hinten durcharbeiten. Nimm dir aber nicht zu viel auf einmal vor. Bearbeite lieber kleinere Abschnitte und arbeite dafür regelmäßig, vielleicht sogar täglich.

2. Möglichkeit:
Vielleicht kommst du eigentlich gut zurecht, hast aber einige Lücken? Kläre genau, am besten mithilfe deiner Lehrerin oder deines Lehrers, wo deine Lücken sind. Sieh im Inhaltsverzeichnis nach, wähle einzelne Abschnitte aus und arbeite sie durch.

GOOD TO KNOW — Zum Arbeiten mit diesem Buch

- ▶ Viele Aufgaben kannst du im Buch lösen. Benutze ein **Arbeitsheft,** wenn du viel schreiben musst.
- ▶ Bist du beim Lösen der Übungsaufgaben unsicher, schau dir die **Beispiele** dazu noch einmal an.
- ▶ Vergleiche deine Ergebnisse immer sorgsam mit dem **Lösungsheft**. Überprüfe genau, was du falsch gemacht hast. Aus Fehlern kann man gut lernen.
- ▶ Bearbeite dieselben Aufgaben nach einigen Tagen noch einmal. Die **Wiederholung** schafft Sicherheit.

Viel Spaß beim Lernen!

① Revision

Prüfe, was du schon kannst!

▷ Mit den Übungen in diesem Wiederholungsteil kannst du herausfinden, ob du mit diesem Band arbeiten kannst.
▷ Führe die Übungen durch.
▷ Für jede richtige Lösung bekommst du einen Punkt. Trage deine Punktzahl ein und zähle sie dann auf Seite 11 zusammen.
▷ Vielleicht zeigt dein Ergebnis, dass du besser erst einmal den Stoff von Klasse 7 wiederholen solltest.

REMEMBER *Conditional clauses* – Bedingungssätze

Es gibt drei Grundtypen von Bedingungssätzen:

Conditional Clause Type I
Der Bedingungssatz Typ I drückt immer eine erfüllbare Bedingung aus (wenn … dann). Im Nebensatz wird die Bedingung (if) beschrieben, im Hauptsatz was dann passiert (I will / you can usw.).
Bei Typ I steht die erfüllbare Bedingung im if-Satz immer im *simple present*. Die Folge der Bedingung steht im Hauptsatz und wird meist mit dem *will-future* gebildet.
Beispiel: If you learn your vocabulary, you will get a very good mark in your test.

Conditional Clause Type II
Man verwendet Typ II, wenn man daran zweifelt, dass die Bedingung erfüllbar ist oder wenn man genau weiß, dass sie nicht erfüllt werden kann.
Bei Typ II steht die erfüllbare Bedingung im if-Satz im *simple past*. Die Folge im Hauptsatz wird meist mit dem *conditional* (would + infinitive) gebildet.
Das *simple past* im if-Satz drückt hier nicht aus, dass die Handlung in der Vergangenheit stattfand, sondern beschreibt eine unwahrscheinliche Bedingung.
Achtung: Anders als im Deutschen darf im if-Satz nie das *conditional* stehen.
Beispiele: Mum, if I won a million Euros, I would travel around the world. – And if you did not dream so much, you would be able to finish your homework much sooner.

Conditional Clause Type III
Man verwendet Typ III, wenn man weiß, dass die Bedingung nicht mehr erfüllt werden kann, weil es sich um eine abgeschlossene Situation handelt, die in der Vergangenheit stattgefunden hat. Der Bedingungssatz Typ III wird daher benutzt, wenn man sagen möchte, wie eine Situation sein könnte, wenn etwas anderes passiert wäre.
Bei Typ III steht die nicht mehr erfüllbare Bedingung im if-Satz im *past perfect*. Die Folge im Hauptsatz muss im *conditional perfect* (would + have + past participle) stehen.

Revision

Beispiele: If Peter had seen Sally, he would have said hello to her. She would not have been angry afterwards if he had spoken to her.
Achtung: Steht der if-Satz am Anfang des Satzes, wird zwischen Nebensatz (if) und Hauptsatz ein Komma gesetzt. Steht jedoch der Hauptsatz am Anfang, darf vor dem Nebensatz kein Komma stehen.

1 Complete the dialogue. You have to decide: Conditional I, II or III?
Caroline and Lucy are best friends. They are making plans for their summer holidays.

1. Caroline: If my father _____ (say) yes, I _____ (go) to a youth camp for one or two weeks. My mother has already said yes. Why don't you come with me?
2. Lucy: Good idea! But if I _____ (not get) good marks in my report, my parents _____ (not let) me go.
3. Caroline: Well, I told you to work harder. If you _____ (not fail) the last test in March, you _____ (not be) in trouble ever since.
4. Lucy: I know. And I don't think that they will allow it. Anyway, where _____ (we/go) if my parents _____ (agree)?
5. Caroline: There's a camp where you can do horse-riding. I thought about going there. My mum says if I _____ (enjoy) horse-riding, she _____ (let) me have more horse-riding lessons here.
6. Lucy: You're lucky. If my grades _____ (not improve), my mum _____ (never / allow me / do) that. She says I need to work much more in the afternoons.
7. Caroline: Maybe she's right. Anyway, the camp is quite expensive. You _____ (have to / find) a job if your parents _____ (not pay) for everything.
8. Lucy: I'm sure they won't! If only I _____ (not buy) the new stereo last month, then I _____ (save) more than enough money to pay for the trip.
9. Caroline: Yes, and if I _____ (win) the lottery, I _____ (pay) for you. But I'm not old enough to buy a lottery ticket, so we'll have to find a different solution.
10. Lucy: I should talk to my parents first. If they _____ (not let) me go, I _____ (not have to / think) about the money at all.

You get one point for each correct answer. **Your points:** ____ /21

1 Revision

2 Caroline and Lucy's trip to London (conditional sentences)

Lucy's parents have finally agreed that she can go to the youth camp with Caroline. While they are there, they will go on a trip to London. Of course, Lucy's parents have some good advice for the two girls before they leave for the camp.
There is a mistake in every sentence. Find it and correct it.

1. You can always ask a policeman if you got lost in London.
2. You could visit the Tower of London if you had stayed for two more days.
3. There wouldn't be a statue of Lord Nelson in Trafalgar Square if he loses the battle against the French fleet.
4. You can always listen to funny people if you went to Speaker's Corner.
5. If you want to get from Oxford Street to the Tower by underground, you would have to take the Bakerloo line.
6. If you wanted to see Cleopatra's needle, you can go on a boat trip on the Thames.
7. You could visit dozens of museums in London if you had wanted to.
8. If Prince Charles ever becomes King of England, the coronation would take place at Westminster Abbey, the famous church next to Big Ben.
9. If you miss the Changing of the Guard, you could still see it later.
10. If the weather will be fine in London, you will really love it.

You get one point for each correct answer.   Your points: /10

REMEMBER — Active or passive voice?

Das Passiv wird mit einer Form von be + *past participle* gebildet.
Beispiel: English is spoken all over the world. This was said on TV yesterday.

Nach will, can, must wird die Passivform des Infinitivs benutzt (be + *past participle*).
Beispiele: You will be informed. Windows must be shut.

3 Translate these sentences into English. Use the passive voice where possible.

1. Unser erstes Restaurant wird morgen eröffnet werden. Ich bin sehr aufgeregt (= excited).
2. Hast du letzte Woche alles für die Eröffnung (= opening) vorbereitet?
3. Ich habe das Wasser gekauft, und der Saft wurde gestern geliefert (= to deliver).
4. Bier (= beer) wird nur in Flaschen verkauft, aber den Gästen werden Gläser gegeben (= to give), um es zu trinken.
5. Denkst du, es werden morgen viele Gäste da sein?
6. Es wird sehr voll sein. Zwanzig Leute haben bereits (= already) reserviert (= to book).
7. Wurde der große Tisch auch bestellt (hier = to take)?
8. Nein, der große Tisch ist reserviert für besondere Gäste (= special guests).

Revision

9. Oh, wir müssen die Schilder (= signs) aufstellen (= to put up), dass unsere Gäste gebeten (= to ask) werden, nicht zu rauchen (= to smoke).
10. Denkst du wirklich, dass wir sie brauchen? Das Rauchen (= smoking) wird in keinem Restaurant in diesem Land erlaubt. Die meisten Leute wissen das.
11. Ja, aber das Gesetz (= the law) sagt, dass die Schilder aufgestellt werden müssen. Also lass es uns jetzt machen!

You get one point for each correct answer.   Your points: /11

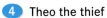 **Theo the thief**

Rewrite the following text, so that Theo is the focus of each sentence. You might have to change active into passive voice or vice versa. Sometimes you do not have to change the sentence at all.

> **EXAMPLE**
>
> The police suspected Theo of having stolen a valuable painting.
> → *Theo was suspected by the police of having stolen a valuable painting.*

1. The police had followed Theo all day.
2. They had seen him leave his flat at 7.10 in the morning, take a bus to Regent Street and enter a travel agency.
3. He came out again at 11 o'clock and they followed him to the office where he usually worked.
4. He stayed in the office building until 7 o'clock that evening and then went for a drink with an unknown woman. They drove in her car.
5. At about 11 p.m. she drove Theo home.
6. The police were still following him, but by then they were exhausted.

You get one point for each correct answer.   Your points: /6

> **REMEMBER** *Future perfect*
>
> Das *future perfect* oder Futur II (auch „vollendete Zukunft" genannt) benutzt man, wenn man ausdrücken will, dass eine Handlung zu einem bestimmten Zeitpunkt in der Zukunft bereits abgeschlossen sein wird. Dieser Zeitpunkt wird durch eine Zeitangabe (By the end of July ...) oder durch einen Nebensatz der Zeit festgelegt (When you get up tomorrow morning, ...).
> Es wird gebildet mit will + have + *past participle*.
> Beispiele: By the end of July I will have finished all my exams.
> When you get up tomorrow morning, your sister will have arrived.

1 Revision

5 Fill in the correct form of the verbs. Use future perfect.
Be careful, the passive voice might sometimes be needed.

1. Mum: When you get up tomorrow morning, I _____ (already / have) my breakfast. But I will leave you some corn-flakes on the table.
2. Peter: I hope I _____ (learn) my vocabulary by seven o'clock tonight. I don't want to miss my favourite TV show.
3. Mum: This time tomorrow, you _____ (write) your English test, so you won't have to work for it tomorrow afternoon.
4. Peter: Great! I really hope my new book _____ (be / deliver) by the time I am back from school. I want to start reading it as soon as I get home.
5. Mum: What do you think? _____ (finish) your book by the time I get back from work in the evening?
6. Peter: Very funny, Mum. But it has more than 300 pages, I guess I _____ (not / finish) it until the end of next week.

You get one point for each correct answer.   Your points: _____ / 6

REMEMBER — *Past perfect*

Das *past perfect* entspricht dem deutschen Plusquamperfekt und wird verwendet, um auszudrücken, dass eine Handlung vor einer anderen Handlung in der Vergangenheit (diese steht im *simple past*) stattgefunden hatte.
Aber Vorsicht! Es wird nur verwendet, wenn die zwei Zeitrahmen deutlich getrennt sind.

Das *past perfect* wird mit had + *past participle* gebildet.
Beispiele:
By the time Louise got to the cinema I had already been waiting for half an hour.
When she arrived, the film had already started. But I still enjoyed the film even though she was late, so we missed the beginning.
Bei diesen Beispielsätzen wechselt der Sprecher von Louise und den Folgen ihrer Verspätung (zwei Zeitrahmen) zum Film und seinen Gefühlen darüber (ein Zeitrahmen). Im zweiten Satz wird daher das *past perfect* nicht verwendet.

Revision

6 **Decide: past or past perfect, simple or progressive?**

Mrs Miller is on the phone. She is talking to her mother.

1. I have a new nanny (= Kindermädchen). She's great! When I _____ (come back) from town yesterday she _____ (already cook) dinner.
2. Oh Mum, I told you. Mrs Philips isn't working anymore. She's so old. Last time she _____ (talk) to little Joseph, she _____ (even forget) his name.
3. Yes, I know. My cleaning lady, Mrs James _____ (work) here for over five years by the time she _____ (retire = in den Ruhestand treten) last June. It was hard to find anyone to take her place.
4. Tina – that's my new nanny – _____ (phone) me right after I _____ (call) the agency. I told her to come that same day so that I could get to know her.
5. I wanted Jim to meet her, too. So I _____ (phone) him, but he _____ (already leave) the office.
6. Tina _____ (already meet) the children when Jim _____ (get home) from work.
7. She _____ (play) with the kids for thirty minutes by the time they _____ (have) to go to bed.
8. The children _____ (be) really sad, because they _____ (like) Tina right from the beginning.
9. When I _____ (go upstairs) to put the children to bed, Tina _____ (already undress) them and put their pyjamas on.
10. She's the best nanny I've ever had. She even _____ (carry) Lucy up to bed when she _____ (fall) asleep in front of the TV yesterday evening. I hope she will stay with us for a long time.

You get one point for each correct answer.   Your points: ____ /20

REMEMBER   *Reported speech*

Steht das einleitende Verb des Berichtens (say, tell usw.) im Präsens, kannst du die Zeit aus der direkten Rede übernehmen. Steht es aber in der Vergangenheit, so wird die Verbform der direkten Rede in der indirekten Rede um eine Zeitstufe in die Vergangenheit zurückversetzt. (*present → past; past → past perfect* usw.).

Beispiele:
Calvin: "I play the piano every day." → Calvin said he played the piano every day.
Paula: "I like basketball." → Paula said she liked basketball.

Achtung: *past perfect*, sowie could, would, should und might bleiben unverändert!

1 Revision

Denk auch daran, Zeitangaben und Personalpronomen zu ändern:
Beispiel:
today → that day   tomorrow → the next day   last week → the week before
I → he/she   we → they

7 Rewrite these sentences, changing them into reported speech.
Ben is a famous athlete. He runs the marathon and he has a lot to tell.

1. Ben: "I'm very busy because I've been preparing for the Olympics."
   Ben said he _____ very busy because he _____ for the Olympics.

2. Ben: "I run 10 miles every day."
   Ben claimed that he _____ 10 miles every day.

3. Ben: "My last competition in March was a terrible failure for me."
   He admitted that _____
   _____.

4. Ben: "But I'm optimistic. I've worked out a new training schedule."
   He explained that he _____ optimistic because he _____ a new training schedule.

5. Ben: "Before I met my new coach I had been training too hard."
   Ben explained that before _____
   _____.

6. Ben: "Believe me; I will never make that mistake again."
   He promised that he _____ that mistake again.

7. Ben: "I was so tired one day that I even fell asleep in a restaurant. That was very embarrassing (= peinlich)."
   Ben told us that he _____ so tired one day that _____ asleep in a restaurant. He added that this _____ very embarrassing for him.

8. Ben: "You may not believe me, but I can laugh about it now."
   He said we _____, but _____ now.

You get one point for each correct answer.   Your points: _____ / 8

12

Revision

> **REMEMBER** — *Relative pronouns and contact clauses*
>
> Who, which und that werden im Singular und im Plural gebraucht. Who bezieht sich nur auf Personen, which nur auf Dinge. That kann für beides benutzt werden.
> Whose ist der Genitiv (für Personen und Dinge). Whom (förmlich) bezieht sich nur auf Personen und wird heutzutage nur nach Präpositionen benutzt.
> Wenn sich das Relativpronomen auf den ganzen vorherigen Satzteil (= vor dem Komma) bezieht (sog. *sentence relative*), muss which benutzt werden.
>
> Beispiele:
> The man who came to see us yesterday was my uncle.
> The woman whose child got lost is Mrs Fawcett.
> School in Germany begins at 8 a.m., which is pretty tough.
> The person to/about whom I was speaking was Mr Fawcett.
>
> **Contact clauses** sind bestimmende Relativsätze ohne Relativpronomen. Sie können dann gebildet werden, wenn das Relativpronomen nicht direkt vor dem Verb steht.
> Beispiele:
> This is the book that Peter gave me.
> He liked the biscuits that I bought him.
> Bei allen Beispielen ist das Relativpronomen jetzt Objekt des Nebensatzes. Hier kann ein *contact clause* benutzt werden:
> This is the book Peter gave me.
> He liked the biscuits I bought him.

8 Fill in the correct relative pronoun where necessary.

1. I like books _____ tell a really exciting story.
2. What's the name of the girl _____ bike you borrowed?
3. Jack couldn't play football yesterday, _____ was a pity.
4. The church _____ I was telling you about is very old.
5. The boy _____ is standing at the back of that photo is my best friend.
6. The country _____ I like best for holidays is Italy.
7. Any school _____ pupils do so well in exams must be good.
8. I live next door to the school, _____ means I don't have to get up so early.
9. I've found the coat _____ I was looking for.
10. Did you write down the homework _____ we have to do for tomorrow?

You get one point for each correct answer.   Your points: _____ / 10

                                          Your total points out of 92 _____

If you have less than 50 points you should look at the book for year 7 again. That will make it easier for you to do the exercises in this book.

13

2 Sprache verstehen

Das solltest du am Ende der Klasse 8 können:

▷ Das Gerundium verwenden
▷ Den Unterschied zwischen Sätzen mit Gerundium und Sätzen mit Infinitiv kennen
▷ Pronomen richtig verwenden
▷ Sätze in indirekter Rede bilden
▷ Das *present perfect progressive* verwenden
▷ Relativ- sowie Konditionalsätze bilden
▷ Die verschiedenen Zeiten korrekt anwenden
▷ Gesagtes oder Textinhalte sinngemäß vom Deutschen ins Englische übertragen und umgekehrt

2.1 *The gerund*

REMEMBER

Das Gerundium wird gebildet mit Verb + ing.
Beispiel:

positive	negative
Betty enjoys cooking.	Betty doesn't enjoy cooking.
Cooking makes me hungry.	Cooking never makes me hungry – it takes away my hunger.

Das Gerundium ist ein verbales Nomen. Es wird verwendet, um eine Aktivität (hier: cooking) im Verhältnis zur handelnden Person darzustellen.
Verben, denen im Allgemeinen -ing folgt, sind z. B.:
enjoy – mind – suggest – stop – finish – avoid – consider – admit – miss – involve – quit – postpone – delay – imagine – deny – risk – practise

1 The theatre visit

Melissa is a theatre fan. She often goes to see plays. Later, she tells her friends about her experience.
Use your own ideas to complete these sentences. Use the gerund.

EXAMPLE

The actress seems to be an interesting person. I always enjoy _____.
→ *I always enjoy watching her.*

2.1 The gerund

1. There weren't any good seats left, but I didn't mind _____.
2. It was a beautiful play, so I suggested _____.
3. The play was very funny. I couldn't stop _____.
4. I hope they keep showing it for another few weeks _____.

2 Translate the following German sentences into English. Use the gerund where possible.

1. Melissa genießt es, zuhause zu arbeiten.
2. Sie zieht das Arbeiten im Garten dem Arbeiten in ihrem Büro vor.
3. Wie du weißt, liebt Melissa es, ins Theater zu gehen.
4. Aber sie hat auch nichts dagegen (not mind), einen Abend zuhause zu verbringen.
5. Was sie am meisten hasst, sind Menschen, die beginnen, etwas zu tun, und es dann aufgeben.
6. Sie vermeidet es normalerweise, mit Menschen zu sprechen, die sie nicht mag.
7. Melissa glaubt, dass Leute, die nicht nett zu anderen Menschen sind, es riskieren, ohne irgendwelche Freunde zu enden.
8. Daher (That is why) hat sie damit aufgehört, schlecht über andere Leute zu reden.
9. Stattdessen übt sie sich darin, nett zu anderen Leuten zu sein.
10. Zum Beispiel hat sie vor kurzem vorgeschlagen, den alten Menschen in der Nachbarschaft zu helfen.

3 Melissa's profile

Melissa has signed up for an Internet chat club. Before she can talk to other people she has to create a profile so that others can see what she is interested in.
Rewrite the underlined parts of the sentences. Use the gerund. Sometimes you might have to change the word order of a sentence.

1. I like to go to the theatre.
2. I also enjoy to read.
3. To watch TV is not my favourite free time activity.
4. It really takes a lot of time to surf the Internet thoroughly.
5. It is important to be nice towards others.
6. Because to laugh at other people is unkind.
7. I believe that to chew gum in lessons is being rude towards teachers.
8. In my opinion, one of the rudest things you can do to another person is not to say 'thank you'.

Sprache verstehen

2.2 Gerund and/or infinitive?

> **REMEMBER**
>
> Viele Verben werden nicht mit dem Gerundium, sondern dem Infinitiv verwendet. Gebildet wird dieser mit to + Verb.
> Beispiel: They decided to steal the money.
>
> Wie das Gerundium ist in diesem Fall auch der Infinitiv ein verbales Nomen und es wird ebenfalls benutzt, um eine Aktivität zu beschreiben.
> Welchen Verben der Infinitiv und welchen das Gerundium folgt, muss (leider) auswendig gelernt werden.
> Bei einigen Wörtern kann sowohl das Gerundium als auch der Infinitiv verwendet werden, ohne dass es zu einem Bedeutungsunterschied kommt. So können die Verben begin/continue/start fast ohne Bedeutungsunterschied mit Infinitiv oder Gerundium verwendet werden.
> Beispiel: It started raining.   oder   It started to rain.
> Hier ist eine Übersicht über die Verwendung des Gerundiums oder des Infinitivs nach häufig verwendeten Verben.

Verben mit Gerundium	Verben mit Infinitiv	Verben mit Gerundium oder Infinitiv
admit	afford	begin
avoid	agree	bother
carry on	aim	continue
consider	arrange	forget
delay	attempt	go on
deny	decide	hate
dislike	deserve	intend
enjoy	expect	like
fancy	fail	love
finish	hope	need
give up	learn	prefer
go on	manage	remember
imagine	offer	stop
involve	plan	start
keep	promise	try
keep on	refuse	
mind	threaten	
miss		
postpone		
put off		
practise (AE: practice)		
risk		

16

2.2 Gerund and/or infinitive?

Es gibt jedoch einige wenige Verben, die bei der Verwendung von -ing bzw. to eine unterschiedliche Bedeutung erhalten. Hierzu zählen die Verben remember, regret, be afraid, help, need, stop, try.
Beispiele:

I remember doing something.
= Ich tat es und nun erinnere ich mich.

I remembered to do something.
= Ich erinnerte mich daran etwas tun zu wollen, und so tat ich es.

I regret saying it.
= Ich sagte es, und nun tut es mir leid.

I regret to say/to tell/to inform you.
= Ich sage etwas, das ich lieber nicht sagen müsste. (Formaler Stil z. B. bei einem Brief eines Amtes).

She tried tying a knot in the rope.
= Sie hat den Knoten tatsächlich (probeweise, als Versuch) gemacht.

She tried to tie a knot in the rope.
= Sie versuchte einen Knoten zu machen (konnte es aber nicht).

1 Put the verb into the correct form, *-ing* or *to*. Sometimes both forms are possible.

Larry and Peter are close friends. They meet for lunch in the school cafeteria daily and sometimes talk about other students. One of their friends recently (= kürzlich) crashed his bike so that he cannot ride it to school for a while.

EXAMPLE

They started _____ (talk) to each other.

→ *They started to talk / talking to each other.*

1. Larry: I cannot imagine Michael _____ (not come) to school by bike.
2. Peter: Yes, it's hard to believe. But I heard his parents agreed _____ (buy) him a new bike soon.
3. Larry: Really?
4. Peter: Well, the question is easy _____ (answer).
5. Larry: Did you know that Michael even asked me _____ (lend) him my bike. He said he hates _____ (walk).
6. Peter: Are you thinking about _____ (lend) him your bike?
7. Larry: I told him that I'm looking forward to _____ (see) him at school, but that I am not willing _____ (lend) him my bike at all. It would take me too long _____ (get) to school then.

17

2 Sprache verstehen

2.3 Reported speech

| REMEMBER | Indirekte Rede bei Aufforderungen |

Beim Bilden von Sätzen in der indirekten Rede wird zwischen verschiedenen Satztypen unterschieden:
- **Aufforderungen**
  Beispiel: "Don't cry!"
- **Aussagen**
  Beispiel: "Red is my favourite colour."
- **Fragen**
  Beispiel: "Do you like pizza?"

Indirekte Rede bei Aufforderungen
Aufforderungssätze in der indirekten Rede werden mit to + *infinitive* gebildet. Im Einleitungssatz wird ein passendes Verb (wie to tell, ask, order usw.) verwendet.
Bei Aufforderungen müssen in der indirekten Rede zwei Formen angepasst werden:
1. Person ändern   (z. B. your → my)
2. Zeitangabe ändern   (z. B. yesterday → the day before)

Beispiel:

positive Aufforderungen	negative Aufforderungen
Mother: "Please go and tidy up your rooms!" (hier: your = Plural)	Teacher: "Do not forget your homework again tomorrow!" (hier: your = Singular)
Mum asked us to go and tidy up our rooms.	The teacher told me not to forget my homework again on the following day.

1 Fill in the gaps. Remember to use the correct forms. Use the past tense.
A group of students is going on an exchange trip to England. In the following excercise, you will find a few things the teacher tells his/her students before they go on their trip.

EXAMPLE

Teacher: "Don't speak German!" The teacher told us _____
The teacher told us not to speak German.

---

1. Teacher: "Be nice to your families!"
   The teacher told us _____.
2. Teacher: "Remember to say thank you!"
   The teacher told us _____.

2.3 Reported speech

3. Teacher: "Don't say that you don't like the food!"
   The teacher told us _____ .
4. Teacher: "Keep your room clean, at all times!"
   The teacher told us _____ .
5. Teacher: "Make your bed in the morning!"
   The teacher told us _____ .

> **REMEMBER** — **Indirekte Rede bei Aussagen**
>
> Bei Aussagesätzen in der indirekten Rede gelten die beiden Regeln wie bei Aufforderungen. Dazu kommt eine dritte Regel: Die **Zeitform** muss angepasst werden.
> 1. Person ändern   (z. B. your → my)
> 2. Zeitangabe ändern   (z. B. yesterday → the day before)
> 3. Zeitform anpassen   (z. B. like → liked)
>
> Die dritte Regel (**Zeitverschiebung**) funktioniert so:
> Steht das einleitende Verb des Berichtens (say, tell usw.) im Präsens, kannst du die Zeit aus der direkten Rede übernehmen. Steht es aber in der Vergangenheit, so wird die Verbform der direkten Rede in der indirekten Rede um eine Zeitstufe in die Vergangenheit zurückversetzt (*present → past; past → past perfect* usw.).
>
> am/is → was   have/has → had   will → would   can → could
> are → were   do/does → did   want, go etc. → wanted, went
>
> **Beispiele:**
>
> | direct speech | reported speech |
> | --- | --- |
> | Tim: "I am feeling great." | Tim said (that) he was feeling great. |
> | Mary: "I cannot take you to school." | I told them that I couldn't take them to school. |
> | Jenny: "Tom has quit his job." | Jenny told them that Tom/he had quit his job. |
> | Billy: "I am going away for the weekend, but I don't know where to go." | Billy told them that he was going away for the weekend, but (he) didn't know where to go. |
>
> Verben im *simple past* oder *present perfect* (did, saw, went etc., have done, have seen, have gone etc.) werden zu *past perfect* (had done, had seen, had gone etc.).
>
> **Ausnahme:**
> In seltenen Fällen kann man die Zeitverschiebung außer Acht lassen, z. B. wenn es um etwas geht, das sich nicht so schnell ändert (Vorlieben, Abneigungen, Alter usw.).
> **Beispiel:**
> Ben: "I love chocolate!"   →   Ben admitted that he loves chocolate.

2 Sprache verstehen

Beispiel:

direct speech	reported speech
Tom: "I woke up feeling great, so I went out for a run before breakfast."	Tom said that he had woken up feeling great so he had gone out for a run before breakfast.
Mary: "I've seen that film already so I want to see something different this evening."	Mary said she had seen the film already so she wanted to see something different that evening.

Im Einleitungssatz wird selbstverständlich ein passendes Verb (wie z. B. say, tell, mention, describe, report, remark, assert) verwendet.

Beispiel:
Tom: "We had a great time at the party." → Tom told me that they had had a great time at the party.

Achte bei der Umwandlung von der direkten in die indirekte Rede darauf, Zeitangaben entsprechend anzupassen. Die folgende Darstellung liefert eine Übersicht.

this (evening)	→	that (evening)
today / this day	→	on that day
these (days)	→	those (days)
now	→	then
(a week) ago	→	(a week) before
last weekendv	→	the weekend before / the previous weekend
here	→	there
next (week)	→	the following (week)
tomorrow	→	the next / following day

2 Fill in the gaps. Remember to use the correct forms.

The exchange students have arrived in England. In the following sentences you will find a few things the students mentioned during their stay in England.

EXAMPLE

Lucy: "I am really happy now."
→ *Lucy told us that she was really happy then.*

2.3 Reported speech

1. Brian: "I didn't like the long train ride yesterday."
   Brian _____.
2. Mr Smith: "Everything has been wonderful so far."
   Mr Smith _____.
3. Tim: "I am a little homesick."
   Tim _____.
4. Tammy: "I don't miss anything."
   Tammy _____.
5. Teacher: "We will tour London tomorrow."
   Our teacher _____.

3 The following sentences are direct speech. Rewrite them in reported speech.

Anne is one of the students who went to England with her classmates. After she had arrived back in Germany, she was telling some friends about the trip. Here are a few quotes (= Zitate) from what she was telling them.

> **EXAMPLE**
>
> Anne: "I saw a lot of sights in London."
> → *Anne said that she had seen a lot of sights in London.*

Anne:
1. "I'd never been to England before."
2. "I spoke a lot of English."
3. "I've got a new friend called Rosa."
4. "I had two host sisters in my family."
5. "I liked the food a lot."
6. But I still don't drink my tea with milk."
7. "It was very sad to say goodbye."
8. "I promised my host sisters to send lots of postcards from Germany."
9. "In the end I even cried at the airport."
10. "I am already planning to go back again next summer."

2 Sprache verstehen

REMEMBER — Indirekte Rede bei Fragen

Bei Fragen in der indirekten Rede müssen die gleichen Unterscheidungen getroffen werden wie bei den Aussagesätzen: Person ändern, Zeitform anpassen, Zeitangabe ändern.
Im Einleitungssatz wird auch hier ein passendes Verb (z. B. ask, inquire) verwendet. Aus der Frage in der direkten Rede wird in der indirekten Rede ein Aussagesatz mit der Satzstellung: **Subjekt – Verb.**

Bei **Fragen ohne Fragewort** muss man in der indirekten Rede whether oder if (= ob) einsetzen.
Beispiel:
Lizzy: "**Do** you **like** chocolate?" → Lizzy asked me **whether (if)** I **liked** chocolate.

Bei **Fragen mit Fragewort** (z. B. when, what, where) muss dieses auch in der indirekten Rede verwendet werden.
Beispiel:
Lizzy: "**Which** chocolate is your favourite?" → Lizzy asked me **which** chocolate was my favourite.

---

4 The following questions are direct speech. Use reported speech.
Of course Anne's friends had a lot of questions to ask her when she returned home.

EXAMPLE

Lucy: What was your overall experience like?
→ *Lucy asked Anne what her overall experience had been like.*

1. Lucy: Would you do the trip again?

2. Pete: What was the weather like?

3. Will: Was there anything you didn't like?

4. Tina: How old were your host sisters?

5. Tom: Where did you go to school?

6. Tina: Were there any nice boys at your school?

2.4 The present perfect progressive

> **REMEMBER**
>
> Das *present perfect progressive* wird mit have/has + been + Verb + -ing gebildet. Es beschreibt eine bis in die Gegenwart andauernde Handlung sowie eine abgeschlossene Handlung, die aber noch Relevanz in der Gegenwart hat.
> Beispiele:
> Thomas **has been playing** tennis for more than two hours. (And he's still playing.)
> "How long **have you been writing** this letter?" (You are still writing.)
>
> Bei diesen Beispielen ist die Handlung (playing tennis bzw. writing this letter) noch nicht abgeschlossen.
> Beispiele:
> "Just look at yourself – you're filthy." "Yes, I've been mending my bike."
> "I'm too tired to do my homework, Mum. I've been playing football."
> Bei diesen Beispielen ist die Handlung abgeschlossen, aber die Wirkung – dass der Sprecher schmutzig bzw. müde ist – hängt von dieser Handlung als andauernde Aktivität gesehen (daher die *progressive form*) ab.
>
> **Beachte:** Bei manchen Verben, wie z. B. know, believe, understand, like, love, hate, owe, own, belong, see, hear, smell, wird die *progressive form* nicht verwendet, weil sie keine andauernde Aktivität bezeichnen sondern einen (oft inneren) Zustand, eine Neigung, Beschaffenheit oder Ähnliches. Manchmal werden diese Verben jedoch in einem anderen Sinne gebraucht, wo sie durchaus eine Aktivität bezeichnen können.
> Beispiele:
> I'm seeing her tomorrow (= I'm meeting her).
> I'm loving it (= I'm enjoying it).
> Is she enjoying her course? No, she's hating it (= not enjoying it).

1 Read the situations and complete the sentences.
Jessica has been living in Japan for a while. She keeps a diary in which she describes her experiences.

> **EXAMPLE**
>
> The rain started two hours ago. It's still raining now. It _____ for two hours.
> → *It has been raining for two hours.*

1. I started writing this diary entry about 20 minutes ago. I am still writing now.
   I _____ for 20 minutes.

2 Sprache verstehen

2. I started my Japanese language class in January. I am still going there. I _____ Japanese since January.
3. I started working in Japan last October. I am still working with the same company now. I _____ since last October.
4. I started writing frequent letters to my pen pal in England a few months ago. I still write regularly. I _____ to my pen pal for a few months.
5. My pen pal, her name is Emma, is travelling round Europe at the moment. She began her tour three months ago, so she _____ for three months now.
6. Emma _____ (learn) a new language in each country she has visited on her journey. She has learnt three different languages so far.
7. In one of her last letters she even asked me whether I spoke Portuguese. I don't, but I answered her that I speak Spanish. So in her latest postcard she asks: "How long _____ (learn) Spanish?"
8. I just received a phone call from my mother. She said: "I _____ (try) to phone you all afternoon. Where have you been?"
9. My answer was "I _____ (sit) in my room writing my diary. I guess I didn't hear the phone. Sorry!"
10. I think I will go on writing tomorrow. I am very tired now, because I _____ (work) hard all day.

| REMEMBER | *Present perfect progressive or present perfect simple?* |

Anhand der folgenden Beispiele soll die Bildung von *present perfect* und *present perfect progressive* zunächst verdeutlicht werden.
Erinnere Dich daran, dass das *present perfect progressive* verwendet wird, um zu beschreiben, wie lange eine Handlung andauert (derzeit noch andauernd oder gerade abgeschlossen), aber auch um die Relevanz einer gerade abgeschlossenen Handlung für die Gegenwart auszudrücken.
Im Gegensatz hierzu wird das *present perfect simple* verwendet, um auszudrücken, wie oft (oder ob überhaupt) oder wie viele Male eine bereits abgeschlossene Handlung ausgeübt worden ist.
Beispiele:

Present perfect progressive	*Present perfect*
Have you been playing tennis? (You look tired but happy.)	Have you ever played tennis? (Otherwise I'll tell you the rules.)
How long have you been reading?	How many pages have you read?
Have you been mending the car? (Focus on the activity of mending the car, which has made him/her filthy.)	Have you mended the car? (Focus on the fact whether the car is now mended and can be used or not.)

2.4 The present perfect progressive

2 Put the Verb into the appropriate form, present perfect simple or present perfect progressive.

Jan is in England. He is with a host family. Jan wants some help with his English. It is difficult for him to understand when to use the progressive form. His host parents give him some examples.

EXAMPLE

You look tired. _____ (you/work) too hard?
→ *Have you been working* too hard?

1. My brother is an actor. He _____ (appear) in a few movies.
2. Is it still raining? – No, _____. (stop)
3. Where have you been? _____ (you/play) tennis?
4. I _____ (read) the book you gave me, but I _____ (not/finish) it yet.
5. Have you _____ (take) the dog for a walk yet?

3 Complete Lisa's letter using the present perfect simple or progressive.

Lisa and Annie are pen friends. They have known each other for a while. Lisa is writing to Annie to tell her what she has been doing lately.

Dear Annie,

Thank you so much for your letter. How _____ (you be)?
I _____ (be) really busy lately. I _____ (not write) to you for a while because I _____ (work) hard for school.
Actually, I _____ just _____ (finish) preparing for a test tomorrow.
Besides my studies, I _____ also _____ (pursue) my personal interests and hobbies. I _____ (paint) a lot. I think it is important to relax sometimes. I _____ also _____ (look) around for another, more active hobby, but I _____ (not find) one yet. Do you have any ideas?
Well, I guess it's time for me to get going. I must finish my homework for tomorrow.

I hope to hear from you soon.

Love,
Lisa

25

Sprache verstehen

2.5 Relative clauses

> **REMEMBER**
>
> **Relativsätze** sind Nebensätze. Sie beschreiben ein Nomen im Hauptsatz näher, ohne einen neuen Satz zu beginnen.
> Beispiel: Tom read a book   which he liked very much.
>   Hauptsatz   Nebensatz
>
> **Relativpronomen** sind:
> which → Subjekt / Objekt für Tiere und Dinge
> who   → Subjekt / Objekt für Personen
> whose → Zugehörigkeit für Personen, Tiere und Dinge
> whom   → als Objekt für Personen (etwas altmodisch; heutzutage meist nur nach Präpositionen benutzt – for whom, to whom usw.)
> which → ein ganzer Satz wird näher beschrieben (sog. *sentence relative*)
> that   → Subjekt/Objekt für Personen, Tiere und Dinge
>
> Beispiele:
> The birds that/which I most often see in my garden are robins.
> My brother, who has been working in France, speaks French really well now.
> Would the person whose car is blocking the entrance please move it.
> Books whose covers have been damaged will not be accepted.
> John, whom/who I haven't seen for seven or eight years, suddenly called me last night.
> She ran away from home. This cannot be explained. → She ran away from home, which cannot be explained.

1 Construct relative clauses by inserting the appropriate relative pronoun.

Barbara Smith, a 14 year old girl, ran away from home because of a stupid mistake. On a radio show the listeners are given a description.

Hello Listeners,
1. This is a special programme today, dealing with a young girl, Barbara Smith, _____ has run away from home.
2. Barbara's hair, _____ she often wears in a ponytail, is brown.
3. Barbara, _____ parents are very worried about her disappearance, is 14 years old.
4. Her parents think she ran away because of a bad mark _____ she was given by her English teacher.
5. The police, to _____ her parents turned the day after her disappearance, have appealed to the public for help.

26

2.5 Relative clauses

6. The bad mark, _____ she received (= erhielt) for not having done her homework once, was not that serious.
7. So Barbara, please know that everything will be OK. Your parents want you to come home, _____ is what we want, too.

> **REMEMBER** — *Defining and non-defining relative clauses*
>
> **Notwendige Relativsätze** (auch: bestimmende Relativsätze) heißen im Englischen *defining relative clauses* (oder auch *identifying relative clauses* bzw. *restrictive relative clauses*). Diese Relativsätze sind notwendig, weil sie etwas Allgemeines näher bestimmen.
> Beispiele:
> The student who achieves the highest mark at school will be awarded a certificate. (erklärt, welcher Schüler die Urkunde bekommt)
> Computer games that involve violence (= Gewalt) are said to have a negative effect on young people. (erklärt, welche Computerspiele gefährlich sind)
>
> Lies nun den folgenden Satz:
> Over there is the woman who/that I met on the bus yesterday.
> Wenn der Relativsatz (wie in diesem Beispiel) ein anderes Subjekt hat als der Hauptsatz, kann man das Relativpronomen weglassen. Der so entstehende Relativsatz (ohne Relativpronomen) heißt im Englischen *contact clause* (s. S. 13).
> Beispiele:
> Over there is the woman I met on the bus yesterday.
> The book that was lost yesterday has now been found. (Relativpronomen notwendig).
> The book (that) I lost yesterday has now been found. (Relativpronomen nicht notwendig).
>
> **Nicht notwendige Relativsätze** (auch: nicht bestimmende Relativsätze) heißen im Englischen *non-defining relative clauses* (oder auch *non-identifying relative clauses* bzw. *non-restrictive relative clauses*).
> Diese Relativsätze werden „nicht notwendig" genannt, weil sie nichts Allgemeines näher bestimmen, sondern nur eine Zusatzinformation geben. Nicht notwendige Relativsätze stehen im Englischen in Kommas.
> Beispiele:
> Albert Einstein, who developed the theory of relativity (= Relativitätstheorie), is considered one of the world's greatest scientists. (gibt zusätzliche Informationen über Albert Einstein)
> London, which is the capital of England, is located on the river Thames. (gibt zusätzliche Informationen über London)

2 Sprache verstehen

2 Defining or non-defining relative clause?

Mrs Miller is a terrible person. Her neighbours hate her because she has her eyes and ears everywhere and likes to talk about everything, which makes many people angry. Here are her discussion topics for today.
Read the two or three sentences and rewrite them to make one sentence. Use either defining or non-defining relative clauses as appropriate. Leave out the relative pronoun where possible.

> **EXAMPLES**
>
> A man showed us the way. He looked like a Mafioso.
> → *The man who showed us the way looked like a Mafioso.* (defining)
> A man showed us the way. He was wearing a yellow hat. He didn't seem to understand us.
> → *The man, who was wearing a yellow hat, didn't seem to understand us.* (non-defining)
> The bus never came. I was waiting for it.
> → *The bus I was waiting for never came.* (defining)
> The bus generally comes on time. Today it was late.
> → *The bus, which generally comes on time, was late today.* (non-defining)

1. A letter came this morning. It didn't have a stamp.
2. Where is the magazine? I left it on the sofa.
3. The boy had twice been caught stealing money. He was seen opening another pupil's school bag.
4. Who was that woman? You were speaking to her.
5. A car overtook us yesterday. It didn't have any lights.
6. My old head teacher must be over 70 by now. He spoke to me at the match.
7. A ball landed in our garden. It belonged to our neighbour's children.
8. This is the dress. I bought it last summer.
9. Our neighbour's children go to the same school as ours. But he never speaks to us.
10. A woman took my bag last week at the hairdresser's. She knows you.
11. Did you find the book? You were looking for it.
12. A man came to the door. He said he was a detective.
13. A girl served us in the restaurant. She was only about 13.
14. My dad retired some years ago. He still sometimes teaches at the university.

2.6 Definite/indefinite article

> **REMEMBER**
>
> Der **unbestimmte Artikel** (*indefinite article*) wird bei **zählbaren** (*countable*) **Nomen** im Singular benutzt. Das sind Nomen, die sowohl im Singular als auch im Plural vorkommen: an apple/apples, a table/lots of tables, a room/seven rooms – sie können alle gezählt werden.
> Der unbestimmte Artikel für zählbare Nomen ist a oder an.
> Andere Dinge des täglichen Lebens, z. B. water, cheese, bread, metal, wood, können nicht gezählt werden und haben daher keine Pluralform. Auch viele eher abstrakte Dinge und Vorstellungen kommen in der Regel nur im Singular vor: honesty, truth, politeness, history, health. Der unbestimmte Artikel (*indefinite article*) wird bei diesen Nomen folglich nicht benutzt.
> Der **bestimmte Artikel** (*definite article*) wird benutzt, wenn das, was vom Nomen bezeichnet wird, klar bestimmt ist, sodass Sprecher/Schreiber und Hörer/Leser wissen, worum es geht:
> Beispiele:
> Could you get me the book I left on the table in the living room.
> Hier wird bestimmt, welches Buch, welcher Tisch und welches Zimmer gemeint ist.
> Are you going to watch the match this evening?
> Hier wird vorausgesetzt, dass alle Beteiligten wissen, um welches Spiel es geht.
> Let's drink water, the milk has gone sour. And let's eat the bread I made yesterday.
> Hier wird bei the milk vorausgesetzt, dass der Hörer weiß, um welche Milch es sich handelt; bei the bread wird dagegen ausdrücklich bestimmt, welches Brot gemeint ist, nämlich das, das ich gestern gebacken habe.
> Die Regel vom bestimmten Artikel hat also nichts damit zu tun, ob ein Nomen zählbar oder unzählbar ist – sie deckt beide Klassen ab – sondern lediglich damit, ob das Nomen etwas bezeichnet, was bestimmt wird.
> Beispiel:
> The apples I bought in the market yesterday were half rotten, and the only cheese they had was the sort you don't like.
>
> Sowohl zählbare als auch unzählbare Nomen können ohne Artikel (*zero article*) vorkommen. Das ist der Fall, wenn alle Nomen, zählbare (im Plural) sowie unzählbare, eine ganze Klasse von Dingen bezeichnen.
> Beispiel:
> Apples, water and milk are all healthy. And health is more important than beauty.
>
> Außer in diesen Regelfällen wird der bestimmte Artikel bei einigen konkreten Dingen des täglichen Lebens verwendet, die ohnehin nur einmal vorkommen, z. B.: the sun, the earth, the moon, the sky, the environment (Umwelt), the sea.

2 Sprache verstehen

Der bestimmte Artikel wird **nicht** im Zusammenhang mit den Nomen bed, work, home, school, church, prison, hospital, university verwendet, sowie bei Mahlzeiten breakfast, lunch, dinner, supper oder vor einem Nomen mit Zahl (gate 10, room 234).
Beispiele:

Nomen gebräuchlich mit *the*	Nomen gebräuchlich ohne *the*
The sun goes down in the west.	I always enjoy dinner.
There are many fish in the sea.	There is no guest in room 12.
Have you seen the moon tonight?	Shall we go to church today?
	Of course you've got to go to school.
	Jack's been taken to hospital.
	Jack was convicted and sent to prison.

Ist jedoch ein bestimmtes Gebäude gemeint, wird der bestimme Artikel benutzt.
Beispiel:
We'll meet in the church at 11 o'clock. I'm going up to the hospital / the prison this afternoon to see Jack.

1 Put in *the* where necessary. If you don't need *the*, leave the space empty.

1. Tina spends a lot of time watching _____ TV.
2. Jodie lay down on _____ sofa and looked at _____ picture on _____ wall.
3. Have you had _____ breakfast yet?
4. Trevor and I arrived at _____ zoo at _____ same time.
5. _____ sun is a star.
6. London is _____ capital of England.
7. _____ royal family lives in _____ Buckingham Palace.
8. Where is _____ room 234, please?
9. Our plane leaves from _____ gate 10.
10. She was wearing _____ hat she bought yesterday.

2 *A/an, the* or no article? Put in the correct answer.

1. Jodie: "This is _____ beautiful house, Joanne. Has it got _____ garden?"
2. Joanne: "Yes, but it's _____ pity, that _____ garden is so small."
3. Jodie: "What's _____ name of _____ pink flower over there?"
4. Joanne: "It has got _____ French name, but I've forgotten it."
5. Jodie: "Oh, you've even got _____ apple tree?"
6. Joanne: "Yes, of course. _____ apples are delicious. You should try one."
7. Jodie: "I'd love to. Thanks. Did you learn _____ gardening at university?"
8. Joanne: "No, at _____ gardening school. Do you go to university?"
9. Jodie: "No, I don't. There isn't _____ university where I live."

2.7 Mediation

> **REMEMBER**
>
> *Mediation* oder **Sprachmittlung** bedeutet, dass du englische Texte im Deutschen sinngemäß wiedergeben kannst und umgekehrt. Dabei geht es weniger um eine wörtliche Übersetzung als um das Wiedergeben wichtiger Inhalte.
> Hier sind einige gute Tipps für die *Mediation*:
> ▶ Du kannst einen längeren Satz leichter in die andere Sprache übertragen, wenn du ihn in mehrere kürzere Sätze unterteilst.
> ▶ Wenn du ein Wort nicht weißt, kannst du es umschreiben.
> ▶ Denk an die Unterschiede zwischen dem Deutschen und dem Englischen (z. B. Wortstellung, Präpositionen, Zeitformen).
> ▶ Du kannst nicht immer Wort für Wort übersetzen. Achte darauf, dass du den Sinn nicht änderst.

1 Can they take it?

You are on an exchange trip to America. You are on your way to your host family in California, but at the moment you have to wait for your connecting flight at Chicago Airport.
Look at the list of things you may (✔) or musn't (✘) take in your hand luggage on a flight.
- ✘ all kinds of drinks
- ✔ baby milk
- ✘ baseball bats, golf clubs and hockey sticks
- ✔ camcorders and cameras
- ✘ deodorants in a spray bottle
- ✔ hairstyling spray
- ✘ knives and scissors
- ✔ laptop computers, video games and mobile phones
- ✘ perfumes and colognes
- ✘ toothpaste
- ✔ umbrellas and walking sticks

A family from Germany is sitting next to you. They do not speak English and are confused about the regulations. They do not know what they can take on board the plane. Help them by explaining to them in German what they have to do.

1. Mutter: Guten Tag. Sprichst du Englisch? Wir fliegen heute zurück nach Deutschland und sind ganz verwirrt. Ich habe ein kleines Baby, dem ich alle vier Stunden die Flasche geben muss. Aber ich weiß gar nicht mehr ob ich das Fläschchen mit an Bord nehmen darf. Getränke sind doch eigentlich verboten, oder? Und stimmt es, dass ich

31

2 Sprache verstehen

mein Parfüm gar nicht in der Handtasche haben darf? Ich weiß, das steht alles auf diesem Flugblatt hier, aber ich verstehe es nicht. Kannst du mir vielleicht helfen?

2. Opa: Carolin, ich weigere mich, mich in einen dieser Leihrollstühle zu setzen. Ich muss doch meinen Stock behalten dürfen, das gibt es doch gar nicht. Immer diese unnützen Regeln. Das nächste mal fahren wir wieder mit dem Auto in den Schwarzwald!

3. Vater: Hat jemand Durst? Ich habe eben extra noch eine große Flasche Wasser gekauft. Die müsste für uns alle den ganzen Flug über reichen. Wir schlafen ja auch noch ein paar Stunden im Flugzeug. Schatz, hast du eigentlich meine Zahnpasta in deiner Handtasche? Du weißt doch, dass ich schlechte Laune bekomme, wenn ich nach dem Aufwachen meine Zähne nicht putzen kann.

4. Sohn: Stellt euch mal alle nebeneinander, ich will noch ein Foto machen. Bestimmt kann man von oben auch ganz toll fotografieren.
Mutter: Lukas, ich weiß gar nicht ob du den Fotoapparat mitnehmen darfst. Und dein Computerspiel müssen wir vielleicht auch in den Koffer packen.
Sohn: Das ist gemein, wenn der Papa seinen Laptop mitnehmen darf, dann will ich auch mein Computerspiel haben.

2.7 Mediation

2 The German newspaper

You are still sitting in the departures hall at the airport. You are reading a German newspaper when suddenly the young man sitting next to you asks you about the article you are reading at the moment. He has seen the picture and is now very interested in the topic. Unfortunately he is American and does not speak German. Read the following article.

Wenn neben dem Unterricht keine Zeit mehr zum Spielen bleibt
Vom harten Leben der Elite-Kinder in China

Der Unterrichtsraum vor uns ist voller Kinder. Alle sehen unglaublich müde aus und können sich kaum noch auf ihren Stühlen halten. Es ist bereits 9 Uhr abends und die meisten der Kinder haben noch zwei Stunden Unterricht vor sich, bevor sie nach Hause gehen dürfen.

5 Wir befinden uns in einer der zahlreichen chinesischen Privatschulen, die die Kinder der Elite abends – nach der eigentlichen Schule – besuchen, um ihre Chancen zu erhöhen, später auf eine Universität gehen zu können.

Selbst die chinesische Regierung, die den Bildungswahn in den letzten Jahren nicht nur gefördert, sondern gar gefordert hat, muss nun einsehen, dass einige Eltern und
10 Privatschulen mittlerweile zu weit gehen. Politiker überlegen derzeit, Abendschulen zu verbieten, die später als 22 Uhr Unterricht an Kinder unter 16 Jahren erteilen. Momentan gehen viele chinesische Kinder nach dem Besuch ihrer Ganztagsschule in eine dieser Abendschulen, die von 18 Uhr bis 22 oder 23 Uhr den Stoff der Regelschulen aufarbeiten und vertiefen. Zeit zum Spielen, Ausruhen oder gar Schlafen bleibt da kaum
15 noch.

„Ich bin immer sehr müde. Bis ich nach dem Abendunterricht zuhause ankomme und im Bett liege, ist es meistens bereits kurz vor Mitternacht.", berichtet ein 15-jähriger Junge. „Dann bin ich morgens in der Schule müde und kann schlecht aufpassen. Dafür muss ich abends dann wieder in die Abendschule, damit ich im Unterricht am nächsten
20 Morgen noch mitkommen kann." Was der Junge hier beschreibt, erscheint wie ein Teufelskreis.

Aber die Konkurrenz ist groß an Chinas Universitäten. Wer hoch hinaus will, muss eben einen Preis dafür bezahlen. Der ist auch für die Eltern hoch, kostet die Abendschule doch immerhin fast 200 pro Woche.
25 „Wir geben die Hälfte unseres Einkommens für die Bildung unseres Sohnes aus.", sagt eine Mutter, die gerade ihren Sprössling von der Abendschule abholt. „Wir verzichten eben auf Urlaub, um die Abendschule finanzieren zu können." Und damit ist diese Familie anscheinend nicht allein. Tatsächlich zeigt eine aktuelle Studie, dass lediglich 20 Prozent aller chinesischer Kinder nicht eine dieser Abendschulen besuchen. Diese
30 20 Prozent haben entweder Eltern, die so arm sind, dass sie sich das Schulgeld nicht leisten können, oder gehören zu den Glücklichen, die so klug sind, dass sie die Extraschulstunden nicht nötig haben.

2 Sprache verstehen

Das System der privaten Zusatzschulen ist mittlerweile so etabliert, dass viele staatliche Schulen Lehrplanthemen aus Zeitgründen sogar komplett wegfallen lassen. Sie können ja sicher sein, dass die Kinder den Stoff trotzdem lernen – in der Abendschule.

35

3 Underline the most important facts and words.
Then write down what you could tell the young American. Express in your own words what the article says.

4 A visitor from Germany

You have finally reached your host family in California and have been staying with them for a couple of weeks now. Yesterday your best friend Dirk came to visit you. You are having a meal together with your guest family and of course they want to know a lot about Dirk. But Dirk's English is not very good, so you have to translate for him.

Translate into German what the family says. Then report Dirk's answer to the guest family. You do not have to translate word by word.

1. Father: So, what did you do before you arrived here, Dirk?
   You:

   Dirk: Also, zuerst war ich drei Tage in New York. Dort habe ich Sightseeing gemacht, habe mir die Freiheitsstatue angesehen, den Central Park usw. Danach habe ich eine Woche lang meine Tante in Miami besucht. Die spricht glücklicherweise Deutsch, darüber bin ich sehr froh, denn sonst hätte ich echt ein Problem gehabt.
   You:

2. Mother: Oh, Miami. I've never been there but I imagine it must be really nice. Did you go to the beach there?
   You:

   Dirk: Ja, aber nur an einem Tag. Ich hatte das Gefühl, dass hauptsächlich alte Menschen in Miami leben. Vielleicht bin ich aber auch einfach nur zur falschen Zeit da gewesen. Die Ferien haben ja noch nirgends angefangen.
   You:

2.7 Mediation

3. Father: And how do you like it in California, so far? Do you think it is very different from where you come from in Germany?
You:

Dirk: Nun, alles scheint hier viel größer zu sein. Die Straßen sind breiter, die Häuser sind höher, es ist viel lauter in der Stadt und ich glaube, dass ich noch nie zuvor so viele Menschen auf einem Haufen gesehen habe. Aber das ist wohl in großen deutschen Städten wie Berlin auch so. Ich komme vom Land, da bin ich das nicht so gewöhnt.
You:

4. Mother: And what are you planning to see while you are here? San Francisco is such a big city, there are so many things worth seeing!
You:

Dirk: Nun, ich würde mir sehr gerne die Golden Gate Brücke ansehen. Ich habe sie schon oft im Fernsehen gesehen und glaube, dass es aufregend ist, sie auch mal in Wirklichkeit zu sehen. Außerdem will ich mir auch eine Fahrt mit dem Cable Car nicht entgehen lassen. Ansonsten will ich einfach viel herumlaufen und fotografieren. Hauptsache, das Wetter ist gut!
You:

2 Sprache verstehen

5 A German Internet text

Your American host brother has to give a presentation about the German school system at his high school. Unfortunately the only Internet text he has found about the topic is written in German. You have promised to help him. Read the article and underline the most important facts and words.

Das deutsche Schulsystem

Alle Schülerinnen und Schüler beginnen ihr Schulleben in Deutschland in der Grundschule. Diese geht von der ersten bis zur vierten Klasse. Normalerweise sind deutsche Kinder bei der Einschulung etwa sechs Jahre alt. Die meisten Schulen bemühen sich, nicht mehr als 30 Kinder in einer Grundschulklasse gleichzeitig zu unterrichten. Neben dem Lesen- und Schreibenlernen stehen Mathematik, Sachkundeunterricht, Sport, Kunst und Religion auf dem Stundenplan. Anders als in der weiterführenden Schule haben Grundschüler meist einen Lehrer oder eine Lehrerin, der oder die die Hauptfächer und einige Nebenfächer in der Klasse unterrichtet. Lediglich Fächer wie Kunst, Religion oder Sport werden oft von anderen Lehrern als dem Klassenlehrer unterrichtet.

Der Religionsunterricht ist an deutschen Schulen konfessionsgebunden zu unterrichten. Dies ist sogar im Grundgesetz der Bundesrepublik Deutschland verankert. Das heißt, dass Kinder je nach ihrer Konfessionszugehörigkeit in Gruppen aufgeteilt und unterrichtet werden. Evangelisch getaufte Kinder gehen in den evangelischen, katholische Kinder in den katholischen Religionsunterricht. An vielen Schulen gibt es auch eine Ethikklasse für Schüler anderer Religionen und Religionslose. Im Ethikunterricht werden hauptsächlich moralische Werte vermittelt.

In vielen deutschen Grundschulen wird bereits ab der zweiten, spätestens aber ab der vierten Grundschulklasse mit dem Englischunterricht begonnen. Da die Kinder zunächst jedoch besonders in der deutschen Rechtschreibung sicher werden sollen, wird im Englischunterricht der Grundschule eher Wert auf das Sprechen gelegt. So werden englische Lieder gesungen, aber auch erste Sätze gesprochen und Namen von Gegenständen gelernt. Die richtige englische Schreibweise und Grammatik wird erst in den weiterführenden Schulen vermittelt.

Am Ende der Grundschule bekommt jeder Schüler eine Empfehlung für die weiterführende Schule. Sehr guten Schülern wird meist empfohlen, das Gymnasium zu besuchen. Schwächere Schüler erhalten Empfehlungen für Realschule oder Hauptschule. Auch wenn diese Empfehlungen nicht in jedem Bundesland verpflichtend sind, sind sie dennoch in den meisten Fällen sinnvoll. Ist das Niveau einer Schule zu hoch für den Schüler, kann dieser schnell unmotiviert werden, was dann zu einem Leistungsabfall führt.

Das Gymnasium dauert je nach Bundesland zwischen acht und neun Jahren. Es wird mit dem Abitur abgeschlossen. Nach der neunten Klasse besitzt ein Gymnasiast den Hauptschulabschluss, nach der zehnten Klasse den Realschulabschluss und nach der vollendeten zwölften Klasse in der Regel die Fachhochschulreife. Dies ermöglicht es den Jugendlichen, auch ohne Abitur in der Tasche an einer Fachhochschule zu studieren.

2.7 Mediation

Anders als in Haupt- oder Realschule muss jeder Schüler eines normalen Gymnasiums zwei Fremdsprachen erlernen. Dies sind Englisch, Französisch, Latein, Altgriechisch, Spanisch oder Italienisch, je nach dem Angebot der Schule. Die meisten Schüler lernen als erste Fremdsprache Englisch, Französisch oder Latein.

Die Realschule endet nach dem zehnten Schuljahr (die vier Grundschuljahre mit eingerechnet). Hier müssen die Schüler, um den Realschulabschluss zu erhalten, am Ende ihrer Schulzeit eine Prüfung ablegen. Im Gegensatz zum Gymnasium muss an dieser Schule lediglich eine Fremdsprache erlernt werden. Es ist jedoch möglich, zusätzlich eine zweite Fremdsprache zu erlernen, was einem guten Schüler nach der zehnten Klasse die Möglichkeit bietet, an ein Gymnasium zu wechseln, um dort nach drei weiteren Schuljahren das Abitur zu machen.

Auch in der Hauptschule wird nur eine Fremdsprache erlernt. Der Hauptschulabschluss wird ebenfalls durch eine Prüfung im letzten Schuljahr abgelegt. Nur wer die Prüfung besteht, verlässt die Schule mit einem Abschlusszeugnis.

Im Gegensatz zum Gymnasium sind die Unterrichtsinhalte auf Haupt- und Realschule weniger komplex. Den Schülern wird hier mehr Zeit und mehr Hilfestellung gegeben, um die Inhalte der einzelnen Fächer zu erlernen.

Ein weiterer Unterschied zwischen Haupt- und Realschule auf der einen und Gymnasium auf der anderen Seite liegt darin, dass Gymnasiasten grundsätzlich klassenweise Unterricht in den einzelnen Fächern erhalten. In einigen Bundesländern gibt es in Haupt- und Realschulen für die Hauptfächer jeweils A- und B-Kurse. Ist ein Schüler beispielsweise in Englisch gut, wird er in diesem Fach zusammen mit anderen Schülern, denen Englisch liegt, in einem A-Kurs unterrichtet. In A-Kursen sind das Tempo und der Anspruch höher. So langweilen sich lernstärkere Schüler nicht so leicht, da die Inhalte seltener wiederholt werden müssen. Der gleiche Schüler kann jedoch beispielsweise in Mathematik eine Schwäche haben. Während er also in Englisch den A-Kurs besucht, geht er in den Mathematikstunden zusammen mit weiteren Schülern in den Mathe-B-Kurs, während die Mathe-Asse seiner Klasse im Mathe A-Kurs lernen. In den B-Kursen ist das Lerntempo langsamer. Die Inhalte werden ausführlicher vom Lehrer erklärt und durch viele Wiederholungen eingeübt. So können die individuellen Stärken jedes Schülers gefördert werden.

Neben diesem so genannten dreigliedrigen Schulsystem (Hauptschule, Realschule, Gymnasium) gibt es in Deutschland auch Gesamtschulen, die alle drei Schultypen in sich vereinen. Das Prinzip ähnelt in etwa den oben genannten A- und B-Kursen. So gibt es an Gesamtschulen in den Hauptfächern Klassen auf Hauptschul-, Realschul- und Gymnasialniveau. Je nach Begabung werden die Schüler jeweils für ein Schulhalbjahr den Kursen zugeteilt. Am Ende der neunten Klasse kann sich ein guter Schüler dafür entscheiden, die zehnte Klasse zu besuchen. Nach der zehnten Klasse kann man sich so auch für die Fachhochschulreife oder das Abitur qualifizieren. Der Vorteil der Gesamtschule liegt darin, dass nicht extra ein Schulwechsel nötig ist, wenn sich ein Schüler aufgrund seiner Noten für eine andere Schulform entscheidet.

2 Sprache verstehen

75 In allen Schulformen entscheiden jeweils die Zeugnisnoten über die Versetzung ins nächste Schuljahr. Hat ein Schüler sehr schlechte Noten in den meisten Fächern, muss er die Jahrgangsstufe wiederholen. Erzielte er in den meisten Fächern gute oder befriedigende Leistungen, wird er in die nächste Klassenstufe versetzt. Im Gegensatz zu vielen anderen Ländern gibt es – abgesehen von den Abschlussprüfungen – keine Prüfungen am
80 Ende des Schuljahres. Die Zeugnisnoten setzen sich aus vielen Noten zusammen, die das ganze Jahr hindurch aufgrund von Klassenarbeiten, Tests und mündlicher Beteiligung im Unterricht gegeben werden. So erfährt der Schüler regelmäßig seinen Leistungsstand und es bleibt ihm noch genug Zeit, bis zum Schuljahresabschlusszeugnis seine Leistungen zu verbessern.

6 Write a short summary of the German text in English.
Use your keywords and structure your thoughts before you start writing. You do not have to keep the structure of the German text.

7 The American school system 🔊 **Track 1**
After you have returned to Germany, your teacher asks you to tell your classmates about the American school system. Luckily, you still have a handout from a presentation at your high school. Read the handout and underline all the important words and facts.

The American school system
The American education system is unlike that in many other countries. Education is primarily the responsibility of state and local government, so there is little standardization in the curriculum. The individual states have great control over what is taught in their schools and over the requirements that a student must meet, and they are also respon-
5 sible for the funding of schooling. Therefore, there is huge variation regarding courses, subjects, and other activities – it always depends on where the school is located. Still, there are some common points, as for example the division of the education system into three levels: elementary/primary education, secondary education, and post-secondary/higher education (college or university).
10 Formal schooling lasts 12 years, until around age 18. Compulsory schooling, though, ends by age 16 in most states; the remaining states require students to attend school until they are 17 or 18. All children in the United States have access to free public schools. Private schools (religious and non-sectarian) are available, but students must pay tuition to attend them.
15 In the following description of the U.S. education structure, we will focus only on the first two levels: primary and secondary schools.
The majority of U.S. children begin their education before entering a regular school. Parents who send their children to pre-schools or nursery schools (age 2-4) and kindergartens (age 5-6) have to finance these institutions privately. Children learn the alphabet,
20 colors, and other elementary basics.

2.7 Mediation

U.S. children enter formal schooling around age 6. Elementary students are typically in one classroom with the same teacher most of the day.
After elementary school, students proceed to middle school, where they usually move from class to class each period, with a new teacher and a new mixture of students in every class. Students can select from a wide range of academic classes and elective classes. In high school, students in their first year are called freshmen, in their second year sophomores, in their third year juniors, and in their last and fourth year seniors. There is an even greater variety of subjects than before. Students must earn a certain number of credits (which they get for a successfully completed course) in order to graduate and be awarded with a high school diploma – there is no final examination like the school-leaving exam in many other countries.
The number and combination of classes required for the high school diploma depend on the school district and the kind of diploma desired.
Only with a high school diploma can students enroll in post-secondary education. It is important to know that colleges and universities sometimes require certain high school credits or tests for admission, and students must plan their high school career with those requirements in mind. Every high school has at least one guidance counselor, usually a teacher, who helps the students with their career plans.

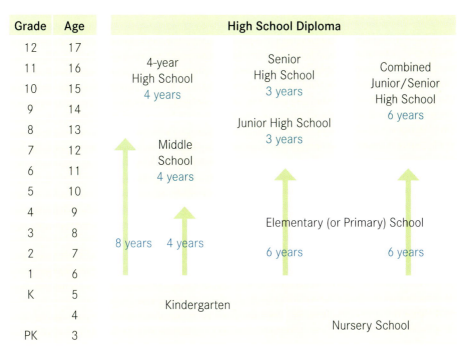

8 Sum up the English text and write a German text which includes all the main aspects.
You do not have to translate word by word. Remember to structure your text.

TEST   Sprache verstehen

Test

1 **Gerund or infinitive? Fill in the correct form of the verbs in brackets.**
Mrs Miller is talking to her best friend on the phone. Here is what she says:

1. Are you sure I lent you some money last week? I don't remember _____ (lend) you any.
2. But another thing. Did you remember _____ (phone) your sister? You told me to remind you.
3. When you see Mandy, remember _____ (give) her my regards, won't you? That's nice of you.
4. No, I haven't found my handbag, yet. I tell you, someone MUST have taken it. I clearly remember _____ (leave) it by the window and now it is gone.
5. Oh, that old woman complains about everything. I think what I said was fair. I don't regret _____ (say) it.
6. I can't go on _____ (work) in that firm anymore. I want another job.
7. No, that's not the reason. But Keith, for example, joined the company 15 years ago. He became a manager after two years. A few years later he went on _____ (become) general manager of the company. And what about me? I've been in the same job for ages.
8. Yes, you are right. The real problem in the company is the new secretary. When I came into the room yesterday, she was reading a newspaper. She looked up and said hello to me, and then went on _____ (read) her newspaper as if I hadn't been there. Terrible person.

You get one point for each correct answer.   Your points: /8

2 **Translate these sentences to make relative clauses.**
John is having a hard week. Nothing seems to work for him at the moment.

1. Er trank Wasser, das Bakterien (= bacteria) enthielt.

2. Sein Auto, dessen Motor (= engine) die Woche zuvor gecheckt worden war, blieb liegen (= break down).

3. Maria, die er bald heiraten wird, wurde plötzlich schlecht, als sie ins Kino wollten.

40

2 TEST   Sprache verstehen

4. Der Fernseher, den er kaufen wollte, war bereits verkauft.

5. Marias Hund biss ihn in die Hand, was für ihn nichts Neues war.

You get two points for each correct answer.   **Your points:**   /10

3 Put in *a/an* or *the* in these sentences where necessary.
Listen to these people's small talk and put in the correct article where necessary.

1. A: Where did you have ____ lunch?
   B: We went to ____ restaurant.
   A: And did you have ____ good meal?
   B: Yes, it was ____ best meal I've ever had in that restaurant.
2. C: Do you often listen to ____ radio?
   D: No, in fact I haven't got ____ radio.
   C: Oh. And do you go to ____ cinema very often?
   D: No, not very often. But I watch a lot of films on ____ television.
3. E: It was ____ nice day today, wasn't it?
   F: Yes, it was beautiful. I went for ____ walk by the sea.
   E: And what did you have for ____ breakfast this morning?
   F: Nothing. I never have ____ breakfast.
4. G: We spent all our money when we stayed in ____ most expensive room in the hotel.
   H: Why didn't you stay in ____ ordinary room?
   G: I didn't want to. I asked the porter "Can you tell me where ____ Room 20 is, please?". He answered "It's on ____ second floor." So I stayed in that room and later realized that it was ____ top suite.
   H: And where was ____ nearest bank, so that you could pay the bill?
   G: Oh, there was one just at ____ end of ____ street.

You get one point for each correct answer.   **Your points:**   /20

4 Keeping up-to-date
Laurie and Kim are old friends. They meet by chance in the city. Put the verbs in the correct form.

EXAMPLE

How ____ (you / are)?
→ *How are you?*

2 TEST Sprache verstehen

1. Laurie: Hello, Kim! I _____ (see) you for ages. How are you?
2. Kim: Hey, Laurie, what a surprise. I'm fine. How about you? You _____ (look) great.
3. Laurie: Thanks. _____ (you want) to go and have a drink or _____ (you / be) in a hurry?
4. Kim: I _____ (go) to the hairstylist.
5. Laurie: Oh no, that's too bad. How often _____ (go)?
6. Kim: I guess every two months. And you? When _____ (you go)?
7. Laurie: Never. I _____ (have) a friend who _____ (cut) my hair.
8. Kim: How is school?
   Laurie: It's fine. Thanks. Maths _____ (be / still) my weak subject, but I _____ (start / work) a lot in the afternoon to get my mark up. How about you?
9. Kim: Maths _____ (be) fine and the other subjects, too. The last time I _____ (speak) to you, you _____ (think) about _____ (attend) a language programme in the south of England. _____ (you / go) there?
10. Laurie: That's right. Unfortunately, the company my father _____ (work) for closed. He _____ (lose) his job and we _____ (not have) the money.
11. Kim: I see. I am sorry to hear that. _____ (he / manage) to find a job since then?
12. Laurie: Oh yes. It _____ (not take) long. And I _____ (be) still keen on going. I guess I _____ (can go) now if I _____ (want) to.
13. Kim: All right. Then _____ (do) it! _____ (you hear) about Mrs Miller's accident? She _____ (die) two months ago in a car crash.
14. Laurie: That's terrible news. I _____ (be) sorry about that. She _____ (be not) old at all.
15. Kim: Yes, I know. Anyway, I have to go. I _____ (must) not keep the hairdresser waiting. It was really nice to see you again.
    Laurie: You, too. Bye.
    Kim: Bye.

You get one point for each correct answer.   Your points: /30

5 Present perfect: simple or progressive form?

1. Emma _____ (always/want) to go to the most expensive restaurant in town.

42

2 TEST Sprache verstehen

2. She _____ (never/be) there before, but tonight she has a date there with Lucas.
3. Lucas _____ (look forward) to the evening with her for a long time.
4. He doesn't have a lot of money, but because he likes her a lot he _____ (agree) to take her to this exclusive place for dinner.
5. Finally, the big evening _____ (come).
6. Emma is very angry, because she _____ (wait) for Lucas in front of the restaurant for 20 minutes by now.
7. In the meantime, Lucas _____ (sit) in a pub since six o'clock.
8. He _____ (talk) to an old friend and the two of them _____ (drink) a lot of beer. There is no end in sight when Lucas suddenly hears his mobile phone ringing.
9. Emma: "Where _____ (be)? I _____ (try) to phone you for 20 minutes now!"
10. Lucas is shocked. He had completely forgotten about his date with Emma: "Emma! You won't believe what happened! I _____ (just/have) an accident. But I'm alright. I will be with you in ten minutes."
11. Emma: "Oh dear! You'll have to tell me everything as soon as you get here. But please hurry up. I _____ (stand) in the cold all this time."
12. There is no need to mention that Lucas _____ (have) a very bad conscience ever since that evening!

You get one point for each correct answer.　　　　　　**Your points:** ___ /14

6 The following morning Lucas told his old friend what had happened.
Turn his sentences into reported speech.

1. "I was sitting in the pub with Robert when Emma phoned."
   Lucas explained that
2. "She asked me where I had been all the time."
   He told his friend how Emma
3. "I could tell she was very angry about having to wait out in the cold."
   Lucas continued that he

You get two points for each correct answer.　　　　　　**Your points:** ___ /6

Your total points out of 88 points: ___

▶ More than 74? Very good.
▶ More than 66? Good.
▶ Less than 44? Have a look at the pages in this chapter again.
    You CAN do better.

43

3 Texte verstehen

Das solltest du am Ende der Klasse 8 können:
Im Bereich Lesen und verstehen:
▷ Längere, komplexe Texte verstehen (Erzähltexte, Zeitungsartikel und andere Sachtexte, Statistiken und Gedichte)
▷ Gliederungsprinzipien anwenden
▷ Wortbedeutungen aus dem Zusammenhang erschließen
▷ Dir Notizen zum Grob- und Detailverständnis machen

Im Bereich Hören und verstehen:
▷ Längere, komplexe Texte verstehen, die in normalem Sprechtempo vorgetragen werden.

3.1 Lesen und verstehen

GOOD TO KNOW *Fictional texts*

Du solltest nach dem Lesen einer Geschichte ihren Inhalt wiedergeben und die wichtigsten Personen nennen können. Notizen können dir dabei helfen.

So kannst du eine Geschichte besser verstehen:

1. *Read for gist*
   Beim ersten Lesen konzentrierst du dich auf die Hauptgeschichte eines Textes und die Personen, die darin vorkommen. Beantworte die Fragen:
   Who? What? When? Where? Why?

2. *Read for detail*
   Lies die Geschichte erneut. Gliedere sie in Sinnabschnitte und finde für jeden Sinnabschnitt eine Überschrift. Markiere dir mit einem farbigen Stift Wörter oder Satzteile, die dir für das Verständnis der Geschichte wichtig erscheinen. So findest du sie später schneller wieder.

3. *New words*
   Wenn ein Wort vorkommt, das du nicht kennst, überlege, bevor du es nachschlägst: Kennst du ein ähnliches Wort? Kannst du es dir von einer anderen Sprache (z. B. Deutsch, Latein) ableiten? Kannst du den Abschnitt verstehen, auch wenn du das Wort nicht kennst? Dann musst du es auch nicht nachschlagen!

4. *Make notes*
   Mach dir Notizen, damit du nichts vergisst. Notiere in deinen eigenen Worten, was im Abschnitt passiert.

3.1 Lesen und verstehen

Mit der folgenden Geschichte bekommst du ein Beispiel für die Arbeit mit Texten. Lies die Geschichte und wende die einzelnen Schritte genau an. Löse danach die Aufgaben. Du kannst dir den Text auch auf der CD anhören.

Tipp: Musst du einen Text wiedergeben, markiere dir nach dem Lesen zunächst Stellen im Text, die du für wichtig hältst. Versuche dann, Fragen zu den markierten Inhalten zu formulieren. Zuletzt gibst du mit deinen eigenen Worten Antworten auf deine Fragen. Am besten legst du den Text dazu zur Seite, damit du nicht vom Text abschreibst. Deine Antworten bieten den Rahmen für deine Textzusammenfassung.

Wenn du über einen Text schreibst, verwendest du immer das *simple present*, denn der Inhalt bleibt immer der gleiche, egal, wie oft oder wann du den Text liest. Dinge, die zeitlich vor der eigentlichen Geschichte spielen, kannst du im *simple past* beschreiben.

Beispiel:
Jimmy, who **is** half Native American and half white, **used to live** in the reservation.

The last Native American's dream 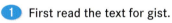 Track 2

1 First read the text for gist.
You can also listen to the text on the CD.

It was a cold morning in December, 1890, but when Jimmy woke up he found he was sweating. Another <u>restless</u> night of wild dreams lay behind him. Something bad was going to happen, he could feel it.
There it was again, that feeling. Jimmy had never known to which world he really
5 belonged. "Mixed-blood" the white man called him. When he had started to work for these people as a <u>translator</u>, he had hoped so much to finally be accepted after all these years in the reservation. Jimmy's mother was a Sioux and had always done her best to educate her son as a Sioux. But he was different from the others, always had been. He was the child of a white man. Just the fact that he was there was a shame.
10 The other children at the <u>reservation</u> had never treated him as one of theirs. He had left the reservation as soon as he had been old enough, but he was still looking for a real home. A place where people liked him, not paying attention to the color of his <u>skin</u>. Jimmy could see it in the white soldiers' faces: they were <u>terrified</u>.
The news <u>spread</u> that the Indians were dancing the Ghost Dance. "The Indians are
15 dancing in the snow, they are wild and crazy", one of the soldiers reported. Jimmy tried to explain that the Ghost Dance was some kind of prayer, nothing to worry about. But they would not listen. The thought of Indian <u>warriors</u> dancing to call the

45

3 Texte verstehen

dead for help in the fight against the American troops scared them to death. "We need protection", the Corporal said and gave the order to arrest Chief Sitting Bull at
20   the Standing Rock Reservation in South Dakota, just until the Indians would calm down again. And Jimmy had to go with them to translate.

Some days later, Jimmy went to see his mother at the reservation. He could see the hatred in the eyes of the Indian people. Something had gone terribly wrong when the troops had come to arrest Sitting Bull. He had been killed in the attempt, not wanting
25   to leave his tribe. Jimmy felt like a traitor, because he was working for the murderers of the greatest Indian Chief the earth had ever seen. Even his own mother could not look into Jimmy's eyes, too painful was the loss of their leader. "Sitting Bull had a dream some nights ago," his mother explained. "In this dream he had foreseen his death at the hands of his own people. Why did it have to be you?" Jimmy could hardly
30   breathe. "But mother, I didn't...", but the old Indian woman interrupted him. "Just before he died and his spirit went to the ancestors in the everlasting prairie, Sitting Bull said: 'I am the last Indian'." She paused, but after a while she spoke again. Jimmy had never heard her voice so sad and grave before. "Sitting Bull was a wise man. Our people are scared and angry. Our end is near." Having said this, she closed
35   her eyes and did not move. Jimmy understood that she had said everything there was to say.

He felt cold and lonely and a deep sadness inside him crept to every part of his body. Again, he knew that he was not welcome in this world. In his people's eyes he was a traitor, because he worked for the white man. The only thing he could do for his tribe
40   now, was to be its voice. He needed to speak up for his people, the white men surely would understand ... they had to understand!

But the U.S. troops did not understand. On December 29, 1890, Colonel James W. Forsyth gave the order to relocate the Sioux under Chief Spotted Elk, who was also known as 'Big Foot', to a military base in Omaha, to keep them under control. The
45   army brought Big Foot's people to Wounded Knee, a place close to a river at the Pine Ridge Reservation in South Dakota, where they should take a rest until they had to walk on. The Colonel wanted to make sure that no one was hurt, so he asked the Indians to hand over their weapons. Most of them were unarmed, others gave their rifles to the soldiers peacefully. Those who said that they did not carry any weapons
50   were searched by the U.S. soldiers.

Everything went well until Black Coyote, a proud Indian warrior, was searched and a brand-new Winchester was found. Black Coyote refused to give it to the soldiers. He claimed that he had had to pay a lot for it and he knew that he would never see his gun again if he gave it away now. When one of the soldiers tried to take the weapon
55   away from Black Coyote, somehow a shot went off.

Within seconds all the soldiers had drawn their weapons. They did not know that the Indian had not shot on purpose, felt threatened and fired back. Clouds of gun smoke filled the air as men, women and children ran for their lives. When the smoke cleared

46

3.1 Lesen und verstehen

and the shooting stopped, about 300 Sioux were dead, Big Foot among them.
60 Twenty-five soldiers had lost their lives.
"I am the last Indian." Jimmy had to think of Sitting Bull's last words. In some sense he had been right. During his lifetime the world of the Indians had changed forever. The old life of the buffalo hunters was over.
Jimmy looked at the beautiful place close to Wounded Knee Creek. The river still
65 went its way peacefully, as if it had forgotten the massacre which had taken place in the fields right next to it.
"Yes, the death of Sitting Bull marked the end of an age", Jimmy thought with tears in his eyes. "But Wounded Knee marked the end of a culture."

2 **Complete the notes.**
Write short answers to the questions.

Who? → The mixed-blood _____ ; Chief _____ ;
Chief _____ Elk, known as _____ ;
the S _____ ; C _____ James
W. Forsyth; Black _____ ; U.S. _____ ; _____

What? → ...
When? → ...
Where? → ...
Why → ...

More information about the Native Americans

The life of the Native Americans (or 'Indians' as they used to be called) changed a lot at the end of the 19th century. They had to live in reservations, which usually were on land the settlers did not want because it was hard to grow plants and food on it. They started to trade with the white men, giving fur and other buffalo products and receiving guns and alcohol from the settlers. Many Native Americans died in the so-called 'Indian wars' (wars against the U.S. soldiers) and even more died because of the illnesses the settlers brought with them.

3 **Now read the text for detail. Find headings for the following sections.**

EXAMPLE

1. lines 1–3 → *Jimmy's foresight – something bad is going to happen* (introduction)

2. lines 4–13 → Facts about ...
3. lines 14–21 → _____
4. lines 22–36 → _____

47

3 Texte verstehen

5. lines 37–41 →
6. lines 42–50 →
7. lines 51–55 → (climax)
8. lines 56–60 →
9. lines 61–68 → (ending)

4 Answer the questions on the text.

EXAMPLE

Why does Jimmy not know to which world he belongs?
→ *Because he is the son of a white man and a Sioux woman, none of the people from either culture really accept him as one of theirs. The Native Americans think he is too much like the white man, the white Americans see the wild Sioux in him.*

1. Why do the U.S. troops arrest Chief Sitting Bull?
   → The U.S. troops arrest Chief Sitting Bull because the American settlers are afraid of   .
   They do not want to hurt him; their plan is just to
                                                                                                                                     .

2. Why do the Sioux dance the Ghost Dance?
   → They dance the Ghost Dance to
                                                                                                                                     .

3. What does Sitting Bull dream before he dieds?
   →
                                                                                                                                     .

4. What happens when the soldiers search Black Coyote?
   →
                                                                                                                                     .

5. What is the sad result of the happenings of December 29, 1890?
   → The sad result of this day's happenings is that about 300 Sioux and
                                                                                                                                     .

6. What are the last words of Sitting Bull and why is he right?
   Sitting Bull's last words are "   " and he is right in the end because the Native Americans were put into
                                                                                                                                     .

3.1 Lesen und verstehen

5 New words

Einige Wörter im Text sind unterstrichen. Manches kannst du dir von deutschen oder bekannten englischen Wörtern ableiten.

EXAMPLE			
restless	→ vom Verb "rest" + -less	→	*rastlos, schlaflos, unruhig*

translator	→ vom Verb "translate"	→	
reservation	→ vom Deutschen	→	
terrified	→ vom Nomen "terror"	→	
warriors	→ vom Nomen "war"	→	
troops	→ vom Deutschen	→	
hatred	→ vom Verb "_____"	→	
(to) arrest	→ vom Deutschen	→	verhaften (Arrest = Haftstrafe, vgl. Hausarrest)
loss	→ vom Verb "lose"	→	
(to) foresee	→ vom Deutschen	→	
grave	→ denke an das Nomen "grave"	→	ernst (wie am Grab), schwerwiegend
sadness	→ vom Adjektiv "_____"	→	
relocate	→ vom Nomen "location"	→	
massacre	→ vom Deutschen	→	

REMEMBER — Prefixes and suffixes

Häufig werden Vor- oder Nachsilben an Wörter angehängt, um deren Bedeutung zu verändern. Die häufigsten Vorsilben sind un- (wie in unhealthy) und in- (incorrect). Sie geben dem Wort eine negative Bedeutung. Eine negative Nachsilbe ist –less (endless, hopeless), die dem deutschen –los (endlos, hoffnungslos) entspricht. Für das deutsche -voll hängt man im Englischen das Suffix –ful an (hopeful).

6 More new words

Andere Wörter kannst du erschließen, wenn du dir den gesamten Abschnitt ansiehst.

EXAMPLE	
shame	→ Der unbestimmte Artikel a deutet darauf hin, dass es sich um ein Nomen handelt. Aus dem Satzzusammenhang kannst du ableiten, dass *shame* „Schande" heißt (auch vom Deutschen: schämen) → **Schande**

49

3 Texte verstehen

skin	→ Du kannst es durch "color of" erraten, wenn du beachtest, dass von "white man" und "Indians" die Rede ist. →	
(to) spread	→ "the news spread" (Z. 14) →	
Chief	→ Aus dem Zusammenhang wird deutlich, dass es sich um den Anführer der Indianer handeln muss. →	
tribe	→ Gruppe bestimmter Indianer →	
traitor	→ Jemand, der für den Feind arbeitet und in Kauf nimmt, dass seinem Volk Nachteile entstehen, weil die Person für Hilfe oder Informationen Geld vom Feind bekommt. →	
ancestors	→ "to call the dead for help" (Z. 17–18) →	
(to) creep	→ sadness crept into every part of his body →	
rifles	→ In Zeile 49 ist von "weapons" die Rede. →	
(to) refuse	→ Im Abschnitt wird klar, dass Black Coyote die Waffe nicht freiwillig herausgeben will. →	
on purpose	→	
threatened	→ Wie fühlt man sich, wenn jemand auf einen schießen will? →	

GOOD TO KNOW — Intelligent guessing: new words

Tauchen in einem Text unbekannte Wörter auf, solltest du sie nur dann im Wörterbuch nachschlagen, wenn du den Text sonst nicht verstehen kannst.
Wörter wie prayer (Gebet), Corporal (Unteroffizier), attempt (Versuch), Colonel (Oberst) und (to) claim (behaupten, fordern) musst du nachschlagen, um herauszufinden, was sie bedeuten. Du kannst aber auch ohne Nachschlagen verstehen, dass es sich bei Corporal und Colonel um Titel des Militärs handeln muss.
Viele unbekannte Wörter sind zum Textverständnis unwichtig, da du die Handlung auch ohne sie verstehen kannst.

Wörter, die häufig vorkommen, solltest du dennoch nachschlagen. Sie sind meist wichtig und können in deinem Wortschatz sehr wertvoll werden.
Für alle anderen Wörter gilt: Versuche sie dir erst von bekannten deutschen Wörtern oder ähnlichen Wörtern in einer anderen Sprache abzuleiten. Halte dich nicht zu lange mit ihnen auf, damit du genug Zeit und Energie für die Textaufgaben hast.

7 "The last Native American's dream" – How much have you understood?
Stell dir vor, einer deiner Freunde kann kein Englisch und möchte gerne wissen, wovon die Geschichte handelt.
Schreibe eine kurze Nacherzählung in deutscher Sprache.

3.1 Lesen und verstehen

The Tanaeka ritual   🔊 Track 3

 Read the text.
You can also listen to the text on the CD.

My name is John. I am thirteen years old and I live with my family in Kaw City, northern Oklahoma. I go to the local school and I like playing football with my friends in my free time. I guess you could say I am an ordinary American boy … only that I am not really American. Or more American than most other boys. I'm a Native
5   American, a Kaw. I belong to the federally recognized Native American tribe which is nowadays officially known as the Kaw Nation.
My grandfather used to be one of the first men in the tribe. He was keen on tradition and told us children a lot about the time of the old Native Americans. "The first Kaw people lived on a small island which was created long before the main part of the
10   earth," he had told us. "After some time the island became too small for all the Kaws, so fathers had to drown their children in the water. The Kaw mothers were very sad and asked Wakanda, the Great Spirit, for more space to live. The women's prayers were answered when beavers and turtles were sent down to enlarge the island from the floor of the great waters. That is how the earth was created," my grandfather had
15   explained in Sioux, our own language. He could speak English but he spoke it only when people were around who did not understand Sioux. With the family he only used Sioux, and that's how I learned it, too.
There is a ceremony in my culture, which turns a boy into a man. My grandfather told me that our tribe had followed that tradition for many hundreds of years. "John, you
20   will soon be old enough for Tanaeka," he told me one morning. "I think it is time for you to learn everything you need to know to take part in it." "What is Tanaeka?", my little sister asked. "It is the time for Native American boys and girls to show that they aren't children anymore," he answered. "John will have to prove that he is a good warrior and can look after himself." – "But how can he prove that?", Emma asked.
25   "We don't go hunting anymore, there are no more fights between the tribes and we buy our food from the supermarket." "It's a tradition, stupid," said my older brother Peter. "Don't worry, John," he turned towards me. "I did it as well, do you remember? And I survived!" He gave me a wink with his left eye, so that grandfather could not see it. But the old man was busy talking to Emma. "The tradition of Tanaeka says that
30   the young warrior or the young squaw has to survive in the wilds without any help for six days." "Six days?", Emma protested. "But that is a long time! Where is John going to sleep? Can we bring him food?"
"Emma, it's an endurance ritual[1]. You have to prove that you can survive without all these things!" Peter explained. "He's right," grandfather agreed. "When I was a little
35   boy, I was painted with the white juice of wild herbs. I didn't wear anything but the white color on my body and I was only allowed to return to the reservation once the

[1] endurance ritual = Reifeprüfung, Härteprüfung

white had gone. I was lucky, because it rained a lot, so the white color was gone after thirteen days, but my father said he had been out there for eighteen days."
"What did you eat?", Emma wanted to know. "Nature provides us with lots of food, if only we know where to find it. I fed on wild berries and hunted rabbits. On the unlucky days I ate grasshoppers and beetles … not very delicious, but nutritious."
"Yuck!", was Emma's reaction to that rather poor diet and I could understand her. Even though the rules were not that strict anymore, the thought of having to go through Tanaeka gave me a sick feeling in my stomach.

My lessons started in the afternoon. I was shown which plants and berries were edible and how to hunt rabbits. I was taught to defend myself against poisonous snakes and which were the safest places to sleep. I had to take Tanaeka at the end of July, so the nights would not be too cold. Children in our times did not have to undergo the ritual naked anymore, but without a pullover or a blanket, I was still facing chilly nights.

The next day, my grandfather taught me how to light a fire. This was very important, not only to keep me warm, but also if I didn't want to eat the rabbits raw. I was a good boy and paid attention to everything he told me, but honestly speaking, I didn't believe that I would ever be able to catch a rabbit or swallow anything as disgusting as a beetle. With each day of lessons that went by, I became more and more aware of the fact that I was facing my worst nightmare. Grandfather even showed me how to make paint from plants, sand and water, so that I could disguise myself in the woods, "in case you come across a white man and need to hide from him," he explained. "Yes, sure," I thought. This was the twenty-first century. Even if I came across a white person in the reservation – which was very unlikely to happen – he surely would not try to kill me. "Just tell him you have to undergo this stupid old ritual and he'll feel so much pity for you, he'll even want to adopt you," Peter joked one evening, when we were sitting around the fire, having dinner.

As the day of Tanaeka came closer, I became more and more worried. I did not sleep anymore and started to feel sick. Even my mother felt pity for me and talked to my grandfather, but he insisted that the ritual had to be followed. The evening before Tanaeka, Peter asked me to help him feed the horses. I just wanted my peace, but something in his eyes made me go with him after all. Silently we went over to the horses. We gave them fresh water and oats along with some fresh apples, which they munched eagerly. We watched them without talking for a while until Peter suddenly said, imitating my grandfather's voice: "So, tomorrow is your big day, my son! Remember that I told you everything there is to know about Tanaeka." The perfect imitation made me laugh. Then Peter went on in his own voice: "It's about time you got to know the secret of the Tanaeka of the 21st century …"

When I left the next morning it was rainy and cold. My mother and Emma looked even more miserable than I did. Only Peter did not seem to be worried about me at all. Two hours later I knew why. The evening before he had told me to hide in the little

3.1 Lesen und verstehen

cave where we used to play as young boys. I thought that was a good idea, so I walked straight to the place near the river. I had given up hope that I would be able to find some dry wood to light a fire like grandfather had shown me, but at least it would be dry in the cave. When I had finally reached the cave I couldn't believe my eyes: there was lots of dry wood inside. But that was not the only thing I found. Peter had put a sleeping bag, some bread and tinned food, a little frying pan and lots of other useful kitchen tools and food into the cave. It looked as if he had spent his whole pocket-money on the material, which would keep me going for at least a week. What can I tell you? I'd never loved my brother more than in that moment in the cave. I quite enjoyed my time in the cave. It was great to be alone for some time. I made plans for my future, went for long walks once the weather was better and I even found some of the tasty wild berries my grandfather had shown me. They made a perfect dessert to the baked beans Peter had left me in cans. I also made sure not to eat too much, because I knew my grandfather would see that I had tricked him if I ate too well. After the six days were over I left the cave and walked home again. My grandfather was so happy and proud when he embraced me, that I even had a bad conscience. For Emma I was a hero and when the evening came I offered Peter to help him with the horses again. When I thanked him and promised to pay him back all the money he had spent on the food, he told me that he had done the same when he had done his own Tanaeka. "Do you remember that I asked you for your pocket money at the time?", he asked me. Right, I had completely forgotten that I had lent him money some years ago. "I never paid it back to you, so I guess we're quits now, aren't we?", he laughed. It was only years later that Emma got to know about the secret, the evening before her own Tanaeka. My grandfather and the rest of the family never found out.

2 Find headings for the passages.

3 Answer the following questions on the text.
You don't have to write full sentences. Your headings can help you.

1. Who?
2. What?
3. When?
4. Where?
5. Why?

53

3 Texte verstehen

4 New words

Below you will find some of the words from the text. Have a look at the lines again to find out what the words mean. Sometimes there are similar German words which will help you understand their meaning. You can look up the words you still do not understand in a dictionary or in the solution pages.

No	line	English word	help	German word
1.	3	ordinary		
2.	5	federally recognized	Federal Republic	
3.	9	(to) create		
4.	11	(to) drown		
5.	13	beaver	water animal which builds dams with wood	
6.	13	turtle	a sea tortoise	
7.	13	(to) enlarge		
8.	21	(to) take part in something		
9.	23	(to) prove	verb to 'a proof of'	
10.	25	(to) hunt	you can hunt animals	
11.	35	(wild) herbs	camomile, peppermint, …	
12.	39–40	(to) provide with	to give	
13.	39–40	(to) feed on		
14.	40	berry; pl: berries	strawberry, raspberry, …	
15.	41	grasshopper	insect	
16.	41	beetle	insect	
17.	41	nutritious	health-giving (food)	
18.	46	edible		
19.	47	poisonous snake	poison can kill you	
20.	49	naked		
21.	52	raw	not cooked	
22.	53	(to) pay attention to	to listen carefully	
23.	54	disgusting	not very tasty	
24.	56	nightmare	a bad dream	
25.	57	(to) disguise	to hide e.g. with a mask	
26.	66	(to) insist	not to take 'no' for an answer	

3.1 Lesen und verstehen

27.	70	(to) munch	to eat noisily	
28.	70	eagerly	full of joy and energy	
29.	71	(to) imitate	to copy, to pretend to be	
30.	76	miserable		
31.	83	tinned food	food in cans, tins	
32.	85	(to) keep you going	to help you survive	
33.	90	dessert	sweet food at end of meal	
34.	93	proud	pleased with someone's achievements	
35.	93–94	bad conscience	feeling of guilt	
36.	99	(to) be quits with	same in German	

5 What does it mean?

Sometimes you cannot translate sentences literally (= word by word), because it would change their meaning. Other sentences have a deeper meaning. Look at the following sentences from the text and explain their real meaning.

> **EXAMPLE**
>
> "… only that I am not really American. Or more American than most other boys" (lines 3–4)
> → *John wants to say that he is not like the other white American boys. But he actually is more American than them, because the white boys' ancestors were colonists from Europe, while he is descended from (= abstammen von) the first people who lived in America: the Native Americans.*

1. "… which is nowadays officially known as The Kaw Nation." (line 6)
   → The 'nowadays' indicates that in former times _____

2. "He could speak English but he spoke it only when people were around who did not understand Sioux." (lines 15–16)
   → The fact that the grandfather never spoke Sioux among people who did not understand it shows that he _____

3 Texte verstehen

3. "... I was facing my worst nightmare." (lines 56)
   → His "worst nightmare" is

4. "... if I came across a white person in the reservation – which was very unlikely to happen – ..." (line 60)
   → It is very unlikely that he will meet a white person in the reservation because

5. "... Peter asked me to help him feed the horses." (line 67)
   → Peter's real intention was to

6. "It's about time you got to know the secret of the Tanaeka of the twenty-first century ..." (lines 74)
   → The secret of the Tanaeka of the twenty-first century is

7. "... I couldn't believe my eyes" (line 81–82)
   → If you cannot believe your eyes

8. "I'd never loved my brother more than in that moment in the cave." (line 86)
   → John wants to express with this sentence that

9. "... my grandfather would see that I had tricked him if I ate too well." (lines 91–92)
   → If Peter

10. "... that I even had a bad conscience." (lines 93–94)
    → Peter feels guilty because

3.1 Lesen und verstehen

6 Right or wrong?

Read the following statements about the text and decide whether they are right or wrong. Correct the wrong ones.

> **EXAMPLE**
>
> The protagonist's name is Jimmy. → Wrong: *The protagonist's name is John.*

1. Tanaeka is an endurance ritual.
2. The ceremony shows that a man is still a boy at heart.
3. According to the legend the island, on which the Kaw people lived, was very big.
4. Legend says that fish enlarged the island.
5. The name of the Great Spirit is Wakanda.
6. Peter tells John that his Tanaeka was very hard.
7. John doesn't like the idea of having to go into the wilderness.
8. That is why he doesn't listen when his grandfather teaches him everything he needs to know in order to survive there.
9. John's mother agrees with his grandfather that he has to undergo the ritual.
10. John finds some wild berries and eats them.
11. After five days John goes back to his family.
12. Peter buys all the food for John and later wants to have the money back.

GOOD TO KNOW   *British English – American English: spelling*

Wenn du Texte über die Geschichte der USA liest, stellst du vielleicht fest, dass manche Wörter anders geschrieben werden als in englischen Texten. *American English* (AE) unterscheidet sich vom *British English* (BE) in der Aussprache, der Rechtschreibung und sogar im Vokabular, d.h. es werden zum Teil andere Wörter verwendet. Hier findest du einige wichtige Unterschiede:

▶ Viele Wörter, die im BE mit -our (colour) geschrieben werden, werden im AE mit -or (color) geschrieben.

▶ Wörter, die im BE auf -re (theatre) enden, enden im AE normalerweise auf -er (theater).

▶ Manche britische Wörter enden auf –gue (dialogue), im Amerikanischen fällt das -ue weg, das Wort endet dann auf -g (dialog).

▶ Viele Verben enden im BE auf -ize **oder** -ise (organise, realise), im AE aber auf -ize (organize, realize). Nomen mit dieser Endung folgen dem gleichen Muster: -isation/-ization.

▶ Im BE werden Konsonanten häufig verdoppelt, z. B. to travel → traveller (AE: traveler), und an einige Wörter wird am Ende ein -e angehängt: programme (AE: program).

3 Texte verstehen

7 Write these American English words in British English.

1. to criticize
2. neighbor
3. catalog
4. center
5. traveling
6. flavor
7. Mom
8. harbor
9. theater
10. dialog
11. color
12. program

GOOD TO KNOW *British English – American English: vocabulary*

Manchmal werden im amerikanischen Englisch andere Wörter verwendet, aber die meisten werden von Briten und Deutschen verstanden, da sie aus den Medien bekannt sind (Film/Fernsehen, Zeitschriften, Internet).

Achtung: Es gibt Wörter, die im britischen und im amerikanischen Englisch verwendet werden, aber eine unterschiedliche Bedeutung haben.

Beispiele:

bathroom	BE: Badezimmer	AE: Toilette (+ Badezimmer)
purse	BE: Geldbeutel	AE: Handtasche
boot	BE: Kofferraum (+ Stiefel)	AE: Stiefel (Kofferraum = trunk)
krank sein	BE: to be ill	AE: to be sick

(to be sick in BE = sich übergeben)

Manche Wörter haben eine unterschiedliche Form des *past participle*.

Beispiel:

bekommen   BE: get, got, got   AE: get, got, gotten

Im BE wird in der Regel kein Punkt (BE: full stop; AE: period) nach Mr und Mrs gesetzt, im AE wird er gesetzt: Mrs./Mr.

3.1 Lesen und verstehen

8 Match the German, BE and AE words.

German	BE	AE
1. Laden/Geschäft	A sweets	a garbage/trash
2. Taxi	B in the city centre	b jail
3. U-Bahn	C mobile (phone)	c intersection
4. Ferien	D class/year/form	d parking lot
5. im Stadtzentrum	E biscuit	e cab
6. Wohnung	F petrol (station)	f first floor
7. Süßigkeiten	G chips	g trailer
8. Gefängnis	H shop	h vacation
9. Herbst	I crossroads	i line
10. Parkplatz	J student/pupil	j cell phone
11. Jahrgang (in der Schule)	K autumn	k bill
12. Handy	L pavement	l sidewalk
13. Müll	M trousers	m apartment
14. Keks	N (bank)note	n student
15. Pommes Frites	O underground/tube	o (go to the) movies
16. Schuldirektor	P caravan	p grade
17. Schüler	Q prison	q downtown
18. Hosen	R (go to the) cinema	r gas (station)
19. Erdgeschoss	S holidays	s (French) fries
20. Benzin (Tankstelle)	T headteacher	t store
21. Straßenkreuzung	U car park	u pants
22. Gehweg, Bürgersteig	V queue	v cookie
23. Wohnwagen	W flat	w principal
24. Geldschein	X ground floor	x subway
25. Schlange, Reihe	Y rubbish	y candy
26. Kino (ins Kino gehen)	Z taxi	z fall

3 Texte verstehen

> **GOOD TO KNOW** — *Factual texts from newspapers or the Internet*

Sachtexte begegnen dir häufig, wenn du etwas nachforschst, zum Beispiel bei der Arbeit an einem Projekt für die Schule. Sachtexte findet man in Broschüren, auf Internetseiten, in Zeitungen, Zeitschriften usw.

Beim Lesen von Sachtexten geht es besonders darum, schnell und sicher die Informationen im Text zu finden, die wichtig sind.
Aber Vorsicht: Dem Inhalt von Sachtexten, besonders, wenn man sie im Internet findet, sollte man nie blind vertrauen!

So filterst du aus einem Sachtext wichtige Informationen heraus:

1. *Skimming*
   Mit dieser Technik findest du heraus, ob der Text für deine Zwecke hilfreich oder interessant ist.
   Schau den Text rasch durch, ohne jedes Wort zu lesen. Suche nach Schlagworten, wie z. B. nach Nomen und Adjektiven, die für dein Thema relevant sind. So kannst du schnell herausfinden, ob der Text für dein Thema passend ist.

2. *Scanning*
   In diesem zweiten Schritt solltest du dir erst die Themen herausschreiben, für die du nach Informationen suchst. Dann lässt du deine Augen Zeile für Zeile über den Text schweifen – wieder ohne jedes Wort zu lesen. Markiere dir am Rand mit einem Bleistift die Passagen, die für dich wichtig sind, oder schreibe dir Stichworte zum Inhalt der Passagen an den Rand.

3. *Intelligent guessing*
   Versuche, die Wörter, die zum Textverständnis wichtig sind, von dir bekannten englischen oder deutschen Wörtern abzuleiten. Findest du so nicht heraus, was sie bedeuten, schlage sie in einem Wörterbuch nach.

4. *Make notes*
   Deine Notizen sollten nach deinen Themen geordnet sein. Das jeweilige Thema ist die Überschrift, darunter notierst du dir alle Informationen aus dem Text. Sofern vorhanden, solltest du dir auch die Nummern der Zeilen herausschreiben, in denen diese Informationen stehen. So hast du gleich eine Gliederung für eine Textzusammenfassung und findest die Passagen schnell wieder, falls du noch etwas nachlesen musst.

3.1 Lesen und verstehen

1 Skim the following text.
Look through this newspaper article quickly to find out what it is about. Underline the keywords, which give you general information on the text.
You can also listen to the text on the CD.

Drugs gain victory over rural areas   🎧 Track 4

"I always wanted to give my children a childhood like the one I experienced myself: playing in the woods, running in the fields, playing with children of the neighbourhood. Nothing to worry about, no cars, no strangers, as long as I was home on time everything was OK." Such expressions can be heard these days from nearly every
5 inhabitant of the little village of Bloxham in Oxfordshire. It is now three weeks since fifteen year old Lindsay Bradford was found in the local primary school playground with an overdose of cocaine. The girl was taken to hospital at the last minute and is now recovering in a clinic specializing in teenage drug problems.
The tragedy clearly shocked everyone in the village, especially parents, who have
10 now set up an association against drug abuse among teenagers. The group meets once a week to develop a strategy covering the following key factors: Observance, Awareness, Involvement. "Facing the problem of drugs in the life of our teenagers does not just mean complaining about the bad times we live in. Everyone has to get involved if we really want to change something," says Larry White, spokesperson of
15 the group and father of three.
Lindsay's story is every parent's worst nightmare and a strong reminder that simply living in the country is no defence against the problems more usually associated with urban areas. The countryside's idyllic cottages and picturesque villages often mask a multitude of underlying problems, particularly for frustrated and bored young people
20 who are turning to drugs and crime in ever-increasing numbers. The sleepy market towns of Spalding and Boston in Lincolnshire were recently revealed to have the third highest rate of drug-related deaths in England and Wales, eleven last year, higher than parts of London. According to the British Crime Survey at least 6% of youngsters in the countryside take class A drugs, only 2% below the level in inner cities.
25 The drug epidemic is not limited to the poor or uneducated, as Lindsay's example shows. Her parents were horrified when their well-behaved, polite teenage daughter became moody and withdrawn and got involved with a gang of difficult teenagers at Banbury Comprehensive School, which Lindsay attended. They discovered that she was taking drugs, including cannabis and amphetamines, and were shocked to learn
30 that she had acted as lookout while the gang stole watches and money during an after-school club session. "Her behaviour changed," says her mother. "Her schoolwork suffered. She started lying about where she was going and who she was with – hard to check when we could only contact her on her mobile phone. She then stole

3 Texte verstehen

from us to buy drugs and when we tried to talk to her she ran away from home. We'd
35 been worried for five days when she was finally found in the schoolyard." The family
puts Lindsay's problems down to peer group pressure and the boredom of life in a
small village like Bloxham, with little for teenagers to do and few people of her own
age.
Drug-taking has apparently become a routine part of village life for teenagers.
40 "A friend's son, brought up in Yorkshire, confessed that he and his friends would
comb the fields for 'magic' mushrooms and that at school, at least half of his
contemporaries smoked cannabis," explains Professor Mark Rellis, director of the
Centre for Public Health at Oxford University, who supports the work of the 'Bloxham
Initiative against Drug Abuse' (BlaDA). "Young people get increasing amounts of
45 drugs information via television, youth magazines and the Internet," he says.
"Once-expensive drugs are now affordable and there is more mixing of populations
through rock festivals and other events which attract teenagers, so it would be
surprising if the overall rise in drug use were not mirrored in rural areas."
A local boy says, "It's no wonder half the kids round here are on drugs. There's
50 nothing else to do!" This is exactly where BlaDA wants to start its offensive. "We
have to give our kids something to do in their free time," says Larry White. "We have
decided to build a new youth centre and many citizens have volunteered to offer
activities such as computer courses, setting up a news magazine for teenagers of the
region and all kinds of outdoor activities. We are also planning to work together with
55 Oxford University in order to offer help for those families who have drug problems, no
matter who in the family takes the drugs. We want to show both kids and parents
that they're not alone and together we can make it. Observe what happens around
you, be aware of what you see and take the initiative whenever it's necessary."

2 Scan the text.

Look at the article again, but do not read every word. Is there any information about these topics? Tick (✔).

	yes	no		yes	no
1. alcohol abuse	☐	☐	5. boredom in towns	☐	☐
2. drug abuse	☐	☐	6. boredom in villages	☐	☐
3. teenagers	☐	☐	7. parents' initiative	☐	☐
4. pets	☐	☐	8. school initiative	☐	☐

3.1 Lesen und verstehen

3 New words

There are a lot of words and expressions in the article which you may not know. Have a closer look at the passages these are taken from and match them with the German translations.

1.	(title)	to gain victory over	A	Drogenmissbrauch
2.	(title)	rural areas	B	Schutz vor, Verteidigung gegen
3.	(l. 3)	to be home on time	C	launisch, trübsinnig und zurückgezogen
4.	(l. 5)	inhabitant of	D	aufgedeckt, enthüllt werden
5.	(l. 7)	overdose of cocaine	E	etwas durchsuchen, durchkämmen nach
6.	(l. 8)	to recover	F	Wache, Schmiere stehen
7.	(l. 10)	association	G	sich spiegeln in
8.	(l. 10)	drug abuse	H	Zeitgenossen, Altersgenossen
9.	(l. 11)	to develop a strategy	I	ländliche Gegenden
10.	(l. 11)	to cover the key factors	J	harte Drogen
11.	(l. 13)	to complain about	K	leiden (an)
12.	(l. 16)	a strong reminder	L	ständig wachsende (An-) Zahl(en)
13.	(l. 17)	defence against	M	jemandem etwas anbieten
14.	(l. 18)	urban areas	N	erschwinglich sein
15.	(l. 18)	picturesque villages	O	wahrnehmen, beobachten, bemerken
16.	(l. 18–19)	a multitude of	P	Einwohner von
17.	(l. 20)	ever-increasing numbers	Q	Bürger, Einwohner
18.	(l. 21)	to be revealed	R	ein genereller Anstieg von
19.	(l. 22)	drug-related death	S	sich freiwillig melden für/um zu
20.	(l. 24)	class A drugs	T	siegen über/den Sieg erreichen
21.	(l. 25)	epidemic	U	die Initiative ergreifen, den ersten Schritt tun
22.	(l. 26)	polite	V	sich beschweren, beklagen über
23.	(l. 27)	moody and withdrawn	W	gestehen, zugeben, beichten
24.	(l. 30)	lookout	X	Verein, Gesellschaft, Verband
25.	(l. 32)	to suffer from	Y	Schlüsselfaktoren abdecken, enthalten
26.	(l. 36)	to put something down to	Z	egal wer, gleichgültig wer
27.	(l. 36)	peer group pressure	a	starke Mahnung, Gedächtnishilfe
28.	(l. 40)	to confess	b	malerische Dörfer
29.	(l. 41)	to comb something for	c	höflich
30.	(l. 42)	contemporaries	d	pünktlich zuhause sein
31.	(l. 44)	amounts of	e	sich erholen, genesen
32.	(l. 46)	to be affordable	f	Summe von, Menge an, Betrag/Wert
33.	(l. 48)	an overall rise in	g	Vielzahl an, große Menge von

3 Texte verstehen

34.	(l. 48)	to be mirrored in	h	etwas zurückführen auf, zuschreiben
35.	(l. 52)	citizens	i	erkennen, sich bewusst werden, merken
36.	(l. 52)	to volunteer for / to do	j	städtische Gegenden
37.	(l. 52)	to offer somebody something	k	Seuche, Epidemie
38.	(l. 55–56)	no matter who	l	durch Drogen verursachter Tod, Tod durch Drogen
39.	(l. 57)	to observe	m	Überdosis (an) Kokain
40.	(l. 58)	to be aware of	n	Gruppenzwang
41.	(l. 58)	to take the initiative	o	eine Strategie / einen Plan entwickeln

4 Find headings for each paragraph.

EXAMPLE

Paragraph 1   lines 1–8   *Village girl on drugs*

Paragraph 2   lines 9–15
Paragraph 3   lines 16–24
Paragraph 4   lines 25–38
Paragraph 5   lines 39–48
Paragraph 6   lines 49–58

GOOD TO KNOW   *How to write a summary*

Der erste Satz einer **Zusammenfassung** sollte Folgendes beinhalten:
▶ den Titel des Textes (z. B. des Artikels, der Geschichte, des Romans),
▶ den Namen des Autors (falls bekannt),
▶ Datum oder Jahr der Veröffentlichung und bei Zeitungsartikeln den Namen der Zeitung.

Achte darauf, dass deutlich wird, dass die Aussagen anderer Personen wiedergegeben werden. Nützliche Formulierungen sind z. B.:
the article states that ... / it is said ... / in his article the author reveals ... / according to the author ... / the article gives the following reasons for ...

Beispiel:
The article 'Violence Rising in Suburbs', written by Mark Jennings and published in 'The Times' of April 3, 2008, deals with the problem of rising criminality in the suburbs of big cities. The author claims that ...

3.1 Lesen und verstehen

Gib den Text nicht zu detailliert wieder. Schreibe für jeden Abschnitt ein oder zwei Sätze. Achte darauf, dass du **die wichtigsten** Informationen wiedergibst.
Denk daran, dass deine Leser den Originaltext nicht kennen. Du musst sie informieren, sodass sie selbst entscheiden können, ob sie den Text auch lesen möchten.

5 Summing up the article
Use your paragraph headings (or the ones from the solution pages) and write a short summary of the article with help from the box above.

6 Translate the following sentences from the article into German.

1. Nothing to worry about, no cars, no strangers, as long as I was home on time everything was OK. (ll. 3 – 4)
2. It is now three weeks since fifteen year old Lindsay Bradford was found in the local primary school playground with an overdose of cocaine. (ll. 5 – 7)
3. The girl was taken to hospital at the last minute and is now recovering in a clinic specializing in teenage drug problems. (ll. 7 – 8)
4. Everyone has to get involved if we really want to change something. (ll. 13 – 14)
5. The countryside's idyllic cottages and picturesque villages often mask a multitude of underlying problems, particularly for frustrated and bored young people who are turning to drugs and crime in ever-increasing numbers. (ll. 18 – 20)
6. She started lying about where she was going and who she was with – hard to check when we could only contact her on her mobile phone. (ll. 32 – 33)
7. The family puts Lindsay's problems down to peer group pressure and the boredom of life in a small village. (ll. 35 – 37)
8. We want to show both kids and parents that they are not alone and together we can make it. (ll. 56 – 57)

REMEMBER — *Emphasis with -self and do/did*

Mit Pronomen, die auf *-self/-selves* enden, kannst du betonen (= emphasize), dass eine Person etwas selbstständig tut, ohne Hilfe von anderen. Diese Reflexivpronomen stehen in der Regel am Ende des Satzes.
Beispiel: Mother: "Why don't you ask your father for help?"
Son: "No thank you. I can do it **myself**!"

Um das Verb zu betonen, das hervorhebt, was die Person tut oder tat, kann man das Verb mit *to do* (im *past tense did*) verwenden. Das geht aber nur in einfachen Zeitformen (*simple present* and *simple past*). Man verwendet diese besonders

3 Texte verstehen

betonten Aussagen, um **Zweifel** oder Unglaube bei der Person zu überwinden, mit der man spricht.

Beispiele:

Unbetont: I understand. The glass is broken, but it wasn't you who did it.
I intended to pass the exam. I studied a lot for it.
I saw Jane yesterday and told her I wasn't going to come.
Tell me if you need my help.

Betont: I **do** understand! It really wasn't you who broke the glass.
→ Ich verstehe dich wirklich.
I **did** intend to pass the exam. Or why do you think I studied so hard?
→ Ich hatte wirklich vor, die Prüfung zu bestehen.
I **did** see Jane yesterday, and I **did** tell her I wasn't going to come.
→ Ich habe Jane wirklich gestern gesehen und ich habe ihr wirklich erzählt, dass ich nicht kommen würde.
Do tell me if you need my help.
→ Sag mir doch bitte, wenn du meine Hilfe brauchst.

7 At the BlaDA meeting

Rewrite the sentences to emphasize the underlined verb. Sentences in brackets do not have to be rewritten.

1. We need a better programme for our teenagers to keep them off drugs.

2. Let me know if you want me to offer an activity.

3. (Didn't you notice that something was wrong with your daughter? –) (Of course) we noticed but there was nothing we could do.

4. Lindsay: I wanted to stop taking drugs but I just couldn't.

5. Cathy: I wanted to call you earlier but you had been so strange when we last saw each other.

6. I really believe that we can change something in our community.

7. Lindsay: I heard what my parents told me about drugs but I didn't want to listen.

8. Cathy: I never believed how dangerous drugs can be, but I know better now!

3.1 Lesen und verstehen

8 Mr and Mrs Bradford's visit to the clinic

Translate the German sentences into English. Use emphasizing self-pronouns (himself, ourselves, etc.) where possible.

1. Lindsay: I wanted to call Cathy but I don't have her number here.
   Mrs B.: Shall I call the number for you, Lindsay?
   Lindsay:
   (Nein, danke Mutti. Ich kann sie selbst anrufen.)
   Just give me her number, please.

2. Lindsay: Dad, can you help me with this TV, please? Something is wrong with it.
   Mr B.:
   (Warum versuchst du es nicht selbst?)
   You have always been better with these things than me.

3. Mrs B.: Hey, your TV is working again!
   Mr B.:
   (Ja, Lindsay hat ihn selbst repariert.)

4. Lindsay: Dad, your hair is different than before. It looks nice.
   Mrs B.: Do you think so?
   (Er hat es sich selbst geschnitten.)

5. Mrs B.: It's very boring at home without you.
   Lindsay: And I am not there to look after you. (Hihi)

   (Ihr müsst euch selbst um euch kümmern.)

6. Mr B.: I beg your pardon, young lady.

   (Deine Mutter und ich sind alt genug, um auf uns selbst aufzupassen.)

7. Lindsay: Did Cathy tell my old friends to ask you for my phone number in the clinic?
   Mrs B.:
   (Nein, sie haben uns selbst gefragt.)

8. Mrs B.: Lindsay, I heard that Cathy is planning to give a presentation about the dangers of drugs at school. Was it your idea?
   Lindsay:
   (Nein, war es nicht. Sie hatte selbst die Idee.)

9. Mr B.: But you surely talked about it, didn't you?
   Lindsay:
   (Ja, haben wir. Und ich habe ihr gesagt, dass ich es selbst nie tun könnte. Ich würde mich einfach zu sehr schämen. [= to be embarrassed])

TEST Texte verstehen

Test

1 Read the following article from a youth magazine. Then tick the right answer without looking at the text.
You can also listen to the text on the CD.

And you really think drugs are fun? 🎧 Track 5

I am sure many of you have friends who like to smoke cigarettes or cannabis in their free time. And I am even surer that some of them will have asked you "Do you want one?" or "Why don't you join us? It's fun! One won't make you addicted!"
There you are then, and you don't know what to do. Maybe you think something like
5   "Cool, I've always wanted to try that!" Or you actually never wanted to take drugs, but you feel that if you say "no" to your friends, they will think you are a coward, a baby or even a spoilsport[1].
I know what I'm talking about: I've had "friends" like that. And honestly speaking, I've considered giving in to them more than once. I guess it's a mixture of curiosity and
10   peer group pressure that makes young people like you and me do these things. I've never really worried about it. I always told myself that it belongs to the process of growing up. Of course I've seen the documentaries on TV. Yes, I did listen to what my parents and the teachers said about the dangers of drugs. But hey, that surely won't happen to me, will it? I'm different! I'm not a junkie!
15   It was last month that I suddenly changed my mind. My best friend Lindsay ran away from home and when she was found again, five days later, she was lying in the school yard with an overdose of cocaine.
It had all started with her new boyfriend. I never really liked him; he seemed not to care about anything. I guess the only person he ever thought of was himself. Lindsay
20   started hanging around with his friends and I knew that they were smoking cannabis, but I never thought they would drive her into class A drugs. Soon everything we used to do together was too boring for her. Sometimes I didn't see her for a couple of days apart from in lessons. She stopped doing her homework and mostly kept to herself in the breaks. She always seemed to be in a bad mood. I knew there was something
25   going on, but didn't know what to do or what to say to her. I even thought of talking to her parents about it. I didn't do so in the end because I was afraid she would be angry with me if I did. It was her parents who talked to me after some weeks. Unfortunately it was already too late. I didn't know her anymore at that point and it was only two days later that she packed her bags and left home.
30   Lindsay is in a special clinic now. She was suffering from withdrawal symptoms, but luckily she's getting better now. We've learned our lesson. Drugs ruin your life. They

[1] Spielverderber

68

3 TEST Texte verstehen

take away your friends and family and – what's even worse – your free will and your personality. I really feel pity for people who believe that drugs are the only fun they have in life. Be happy that you have a life at all. Say no to drugs!

1. The author says ...
   a. she has never had a friend who offered her drugs.
   b. she once knew a drug dealer.
   c. people she thought were her friends offered her drugs.

2. She says you are in danger of being called a spoilsport if ...
   a. you do not try all the drugs which are on the market.
   b. you tell your friends that you don't want to take drugs.
   c. you tell your teachers that your friends take drugs.

3. The author says she herself ...
   a. tried drugs, but didn't like it.
   b. never took any drugs.
   c. thought about trying drugs.

4. She believes that documentaries on TV and lessons about the dangers of drugs at school ...
   a. are important, but teenagers think drugs will not harm them.
   b. are important, but teenagers do not believe what is said.
   c. are important and do put teenagers off (= abschrecken) taking drugs.

5. The article states that the author has been convinced of the danger of drugs ever since ....
   a. she lost some friends to drugs.
   b. she nearly died because of drugs.
   c. she saw how her friend suffered from drugs.

You get one point for each correct answer.   Your points: /5

2 Find expressions in the text which say ...

1. Das gehört zum Erwachsenwerden dazu.
2. ... wenn ich es täte.
3. Alles schien ihm gleichgültig zu sein.
4. Eine wird dich schon nicht abhängig machen!
5. Ich wusste dass irgendwas im Busch war.
6. Sie litt an Entzugserscheinungen.
7. Klasse, das wollte ich schon immer mal probieren!
8. ... außer im Unterricht.

You get one point for each correct answer   Your points: /8

3 TEST Texte verstehen

3 Explain in your own words. Look at the text again for ideas.

1. The author says that some teenagers take drugs when they're offered them, even if they do not actually want to, because …
2. She says she knows what she is talking about, because …
3. She told herself taking drugs would not hurt her because …
4. But she changed her mind about drugs when …
5. Describing Lindsay's change of behaviour, she says …
6. After seeing her friend suffering from withdrawal symptoms she is happy that …
7. The author describes her feelings for people who take drugs as …
8. She says that every teenager should …

You get one point for each correct answer.   Your points: /8

4 Complete the chart.
If you don't know the words, look them up in a dictionary.

	German	BE	AE
1.	Hosen		
2.			jail
3.		in the city centre	
4.	üben		
5.		crossroads	
6.			trash, garbage
7.			neighborhood
8.	Pommes		
9.	Wohnwagen		
10.	Geschmacksrichtung		
11.		cinema	
12.			cab
13.			pajamas
14.	Handy		
15.		shop	
16.			vacation
17.	Süßigkeiten		
18.		petrol	
19.			soccer
20.	Geldschein		

You get one point for each correct answer.   Your points: /40

3 TEST Texte verstehen

5 The following letter is written in AE. Find the 19 AE word/spelling differences and change them into BE in the lines below. One mistake appears twice in the text.

Dear Lindsay,

I hope you are feeling better. Don't worry; we have not forgotten you. Yesterday

all the students of our grade went downtown to go to the theater. Only Lucy

had to stay at home because she was sick. We had to wait in a long line before we

were allowed to go in. Mrs. Peters said it would be an interesting program, but we

thought it was trash. We ate lots of candy and cookies; you know that I especially like

the ones with chocolate flavor. After the play we wanted to go to the harbor, but the

subway was closed for repair works, so we had to take cabs. There were not enough

seats, so Nigel decided to sit in the trunk. Can you imagine the color of Mrs. Peters'

face when she saw him climbing in? "We have to have a dialog in private young

man!" she said. Then she even called his mom on her cell phone. Poor Nigel!

By the way, we are planning a big party for you as soon as you get home again.

So get well soon!

Lots of love,
Cathy

You get one point for each correct answer.   **Your points:**   /19

                               Your total points out of 80 points:

▶ More than 60? Very good.
▶ More than 60? Good.
▶ Less than 40? Have a look at the pages in this chapter again.
  You CAN do better.

71

3 Texte verstehen

3.2 Hören und verstehen

GOOD TO KNOW — *Listening to texts*

Die wichtigsten Arten von Hörtexten sind Nachrichten (news), Radioberichte (reports/radio broadcasts), Interviews oder Hörspiele (radio plays). Richtig zuhören zu können, ist aber auch wichtig, wenn man sich unterhält, telefoniert oder einen Anrufbeantworter abhören muss.

Es ist ganz normal, dass du nicht jedes Wort verstehst. Der Trick, um den Text zu verstehen, ist **einzelne Wörter** herauszuhören, die dir Auskunft darüber geben, wovon der Text handelt.

So kannst du aus einem Hörtext Informationen gewinnen:

1. *Before listening*
   Lies zuerst den Titel des Hörtextes und – soweit vorhanden – die Hinweise zum Text. Sie geben dir erste Hinweise darauf, worum es in dem Text geht. Manchmal fehlen solche Hinweise jedoch. Jetzt solltest du überlegen, was du schon über das Thema weißt und was du gerne aus dem Text erfahren würdest. So bist du gut vorbereitet auf das, was du hören wirst.

2. *While listening*
   Es gibt zwei wichtige Regeln, die man während des Hörens beachten sollte: Mach dir keine Sorgen, wenn du nicht jedes Wort verstehst. Höre einfach auf das, was du verstehen kannst, dann kannst du erraten, worum es geht. Notiere dir auf einem Blatt alles Wichtige in Stichworten. Diese Notizen müssen nicht geordnet sein, denn es soll ja schnell gehen. Wenn der Text fertig ist, ordnest du deine Notizen. Lass ein wenig Platz, denn beim zweiten Hören kannst du dann noch Informationen an der richtigen Stelle ergänzen.

3. *After listening*
   Ergänze und sortiere deine Notizen. Schreibe an den Rand, welche Stichpunkte dir bei der Beantwortung welcher Frage helfen.

Das folgende Beispiel zeigt dir, wie man Notizen sammeln und ordnen kann.

3.2 Hören und verstehen

| EXAMPLE | Taking notes |

British wars → no money → taxes

Acts { Sugar (1764)
       Stamp (1765)
       Townshend (1767)
       Tea (1773)

East India Company

"no taxation without representation"

Sons of Liberty/Samuel Adams/Indians

Dec 16, 1773   Boston Tea Party

throw tea into   ships:
Boston Harbor | Dartmouth, Beaver, Eleanour → unload tea?

→ INDEPENDENCE

British Crown	Colonies	Dates, Acts + Facts
no money after war → more taxes for colonies	need British soldiers for their protection	1764 Sugar Act 1765 Stamp Act 1767 Townshend Act
East India Tea Company → close to bankruptcy	"no taxation without representation"	→ import tax for leather, paper + tea 1773 Tea Act 16.12.1773 Boston Tea Party
	desire for independence → boycott of tea	
no import tax → cheaper than smugglers	Samuel Adams and Sons of Liberty disguised as Indians	ships: Dartmouth, Beaver, Eleanour
	throw tea into Boston Harbour	

73

3 Texte verstehen

Milestones in American History: the Boston Tea Party 🎧 Track 6

The radio report tells you about an important event in American history: the Boston Tea Party. An expert on the topic tells you what happened and how and why. You will also be given some background information on the British colonies in 18th century New England.

1 Add information you can get from the title and the introduction above.
Complete the form with what you know about the topic.

Title: The text is about …
The introduction tells me that I will hear a …
He will talk about ….
I know something about British colonies in New England: that …

| GOOD TO KNOW | *Useful vocabulary* |

Hier findest du Wörter, die für das historische Thema „Boston Tea Party" nützlich sind.

Ereignis, Vorkommnis, Zwischenfall	incident
Schulden	debts
Steuern	taxes
(verabschiedetes) Gesetz, Verordnung	Act
Verlangen, Wunsch, Bitte nach	desire for
Vorrat, Lager, Stapel	stocks of
verlangen, fordern	to demand
Schiff	vessel
verkleiden, maskieren, tarnen	to disguise
Fass, Tonne	cask
leistungsfähig, tüchtig, wirksam, rasch	efficient
(Tür-) Schloss	lock
(Schiffs-) Kai	wharf
Übel-, Missetäter(in), Straffällige(r)	offender

3.2 Hören und verstehen

Besteuerung	taxation
Unruhe, politische Unruhen	unrest
Hafen	port (Achtung! BE: harbour, AE: harbor)
Kaufmann, Großhändler	merchant
Unabhängigkeit	independence
schuldig	guilty
Pelz, Fell	fur
jemanden/etwas unterdrücken, verdrängen	to repress someone/something
Waren, Güter, Gegenstände	goods

2 Read the following statements. Then listen to the text for the first time. Listen to the text "for gist".

For each statement, tick whether it is true or false or whether there is nothing said about it in the text.

No	Statement	true	false	not in text
1.	This episode of "Milestones in American History" deals with the Boston Tea Party.	☐	☐	☐
2.	Walter Peabody wrote a book about famous American tea drinkers.	☐	☐	☐
3.	Mr Peabody says that the colonists had to pay taxes because of the debts of the British Crown due to wars with the French and the Native Americans.	☐	☐	☐
4.	The wars had been so expensive because they had been going on for so long.	☐	☐	☐
5.	The slogan "no taxation without representation" meant that colonists were not willing to pay taxes unless they could send their own politicians to the parliament in London.	☐	☐	☐
6.	The colonists' reaction to the taxes was a boycott of tea sold by the British West India Company.	☐	☐	☐

3 Texte verstehen

7. The tea company then tried to sell its tea from China with the help of smugglers.
8. Because of the *Tea Act* the company finally could offer the tea even cheaper than the smugglers.
9. The price for tea was even cheaper than that for beer in those days.
10. The three famous ships which were lying in Boston Harbor in December 1773 were the *Beaver*, the *Dartmouth* and the *Eleanour*.
11. The *Sons of Liberty* were a group of Native Americans who fought for more independence from the Crown.
12. The incident is called the "Boston Tea Party" because the tea-leaves turned the water in the harbour into tea.

3 Now listen to the text for detail.
Read the questions below. Then listen to the text again. This time concentrate on details. Write down all the information you need to answer the questions.

1. What is the name of the radio programme?
2. How many million pounds of debt did the British Crown have after the wars?
3. Which two Acts were introduced in 1764?
4. Why was there so much tea rotting in the London warehouses in 1773?
5. Because of the new *Tea Act* the East India Company had to pay taxes when one of their tea ships …
   a. entered London.
   b. entered London and again when it entered a New England harbour.
   c. entered a New England harbour.
6. Citizens wanted …
   a. the tea to be sold more cheaply.
   b. the ships with the tea to be unloaded quickly.
   c. the ships with the tea to return to England without unloading the tea.
7. Samuel Adams became famous for having said:
   a. "This meeting can do more to save the country."
   b. "This meeting can do nothing more to save the country."
   c. "This meeting can do much more to save the country."

3.2 Hören und verstehen

8. When the men threw the tea overboard …
   a. they worked quickly and caused a lot of damage.
   b. they were rather slow but didn't damage anything.
   c. they worked quickly and didn't damage anything.

9. Historians say that the most important effect of the Boston Tea Party was that …
   a. the desire for independence gained strength throughout New England.
   b. the British Crown couldn't control the colonists.
   c. tea was thrown overboard in other New England ports.

10. The *Sons of Liberty* dressed up as Native Americans, because …
    a. they wanted to blame the Native Americans, to avoid arrest themselves.
    b. the Native Americans were a symbol of freedom and independence.
    c. the Native Americans were a symbol of war with Britain.

4 Match the sentence halves.

1. After the French and 'Indian' Wars …
2. The solution to this money problem was to …
3. Though the taxes were not too high, they made the citizens angry because …
4. Especially the taxation of tea, leather and paper raised the anger of the colonists because …
5. The *Townshend Act* of 1773 …
6. The British Governor Thomas Hutchinson ordered …
7. The *Sons of Liberty* were a group of New Englanders …
8. The *Eleanour*, the *Dartmouth* and the *Beaver* …
9. The *Sons of Liberty* decided to boycott the East India Company …
10. This event, which happened on December 16, 1773, …

A … these things were needed in everyday life.
B … and – disguised as Native Americans – threw the tea from three ships into the waters of Boston Harbor.
C … raise taxes for the colonists in the New World.
D … became known as the 'Boston Tea Party'.
E … Britain faced huge debts.
F … nearly led to bankruptcy for the East India Company.
G … who wanted more independence from the Crown.
H … the laws were made by parliament and the New World could not send representatives to parliament in London.
I … had tea worth £10,000 on board.
J … the ships of the East India Company to unload their tea at Boston Harbor.

3 Texte verstehen

GOOD TO KNOW — *British and American pronunciation*

Im letzten Kapitel hast du bereits etwas über die Unterschiede zwischen britischem und amerikanischem Englisch in Bezug auf Vokabular und Schreibweise erfahren. Auch bei der Aussprache gibt es Abweichungen.
Wenn du einige Regeln kennst, kannst du sagen, ob eine Person britisches Englisch oder amerikanisches Englisch spricht.
Hier findest einige der wichtigsten Unterschiede.
AE: after, aunt, dance, last or half have the sound [æ].
→ In BE they have the sound [ɑː].
AE: Words like new, Tuesday and stupid have the sound [uː].
→ In BE they have the sound [juː].
AE: The 'o' in words like bottle, hot or everybody is pronounced as [ɑ].
→ In BE they have the sound [ɒ].
AE: You hear the 'r' in words like sure, car, farm or work.
→ In BE you do not hear it.
AE: In words like beautiful, city, better or British, the 't' is often pronounced as 'd'.
→ In BE it is pronounced as 't'.

5 British and American pronunciation   🎵 **Track 7**

Listen to the CD for examples of the different pronunciations. Listen again and pronounce each of these words the British way and after that the American way. This will help you to "feel" the differences between AE and BE.

6 British English or American English?   🎵 **Track 8**

Listen to the following sentences on the CD. Then tick BE or AE. There might also be both in one track, so listen carefully.

Track	BE	AE	both
1.	☐	☐	☐
2.	☐	☐	☐
3.	☐	☐	☐
4.	☐	☐	☐
5.	☐	☐	☐
6.	☐	☐	☐
7.	☐	☐	☐
8.	☐	☐	☐

3.2 Hören und verstehen

Teenage life in Britain and the USA  Tracks 9–14

Herr Meier has organised a project on Britain and the United States of America with his English class. The pupils have learned about the history of both countries, as well as the differences in the language. Now they want to find out about the lives of teenagers in both the USA and the UK. So they have asked two schools – one in England, the other in the USA – to send voicemails in which some teenagers describe their daily life.

1 Listen to the tracks and decide which voicemails are from English and which from American students.
Tick your suggestions in the table below.

Track	British	American
1.	☐	☐
2.	☐	☐
3.	☐	☐
4.	☐	☐
5.	☐	☐
6.	☐	☐

2 Listen to the voicemails again.
Write down the missing names and tick for each teenager all the topics he or she talks about in detail.
Note: If one of them for example says that (s)he has friends, but does not say more about them, you should not tick "friends".

name	school	family	hobbies	friends	daily routine	facts about his/her region
Stacy						
Nolan						
Dean						
D.J.						

79

3 Texte verstehen

Stop: Mistake! 🎧 Track 15

After Herr Meier and his pupils have talked about the voicemails from their British and American partners they decide to send answers back. They want to tell their new friends what life in Germany is like. Because the pupils' English is not so good yet, they have written one text together. Mariella, the best pupil in class, has agreed to read the text out to be recorded.

1) Listen to Mariella's voicemail.
There is at least one factual mistake in each of the statements below. Find the mistakes and correct them.

1. Mariella says that her class found many differences between school life and the teenagers' lives in general in the three countries.

2. She explains that in Germany you can take your Abitur after twelve or thirteen years at school, depending on how good your marks are.

3. Mariella's class has lessons in the afternoon three times a week.

4. The lunch break at their school is between 1 p.m. and 1.50 p.m. and they can have a warm meal at the school cafeteria.

5. Mariella tells her listeners that German pupils often learn to play an instrument at school.

6. She says that unlike British or American teenagers, German teenagers like to spend their free time with their friends.

3.2 Hören und verstehen

2 Listen again and find English expressions in Mariella's voicemail that mean the following:

1. zögert nicht →
2. da es dazu befähigt, … →
3. ich spreche stellvertretend für … →
4. vergleichbar mit … →
5. meistens →
6. es gibt viele Unterschiede →
7. je nach … →
8. bis zu viermal die Woche →
9. seltsamerweise →
10. zum Glück →

3 Translate the following sentences into German.
If you are not sure what they mean, listen to Mariella's voicemail again. Sometimes the context makes it easier to translate.

1. It was very interesting for us to hear about your lives.
2. Especially as far as school-life is concerned.
3. Strangely, outside school teenagers seem to be the same all over the world.
4. If you want to take your "Abitur" – which is comparable to A-Levels in the UK or high school graduation in America, since it allows you to go to university – you have to go to a "Gymnasium".
5. At those schools the pupils are divided into different groups for most subjects, depending on their abilities.
6. We have a different timetable for each day of the week, but it is repeated week by week throughout of the school year.
7. Since we don't have a cafeteria, every pupil has to bring his or her own lunch to school.
8. Oh, and just in case you are jealous that in Germany school finishes so early – we also start early!
9. If you are not interested in any of these workshops you can go home after your last lesson.
10. Don't hesitate to ask us more questions!

3 TEST Texte verstehen

Test

Announcement at an American high school 🎧 Track 16

It is common at American high schools to announce important facts and dates in the breaks via loudspeakers.

1 Listen to what is said on the CD and tick all the topics mentioned in the announcement.

	Topic	Yes	No
1.	Birthday congratulations		
2.	Principal's complaints about students' behavior		
3.	Mother looking for child		
4.	Party preparations of older students		
5.	Opening times of 'lost and found' office		
6.	Results of school team in knowledge competition		
7.	Extra meeting times for clubs because of a special event		
8.	Search for students that should be in class		

You get one point for each correct answer.   Your points: / 8

2 Listen to the announcement again and tick the right answers.

1. The announcement is made on a …
   A Thursday   B Friday   C Saturday

2. The football match against the Dilling High Deltas starts on…
   A Friday at 6 p.m.   B Saturday at 5 p.m.   C Saturday at 6 p.m.

3. Stacy reminds her girls …
   A to miss the cheerleading practice.
   B to practice cheerleading at home.
   C not to miss the cheerleading practice.

4. Who will be waiting for the football team on the field at 5 p.m. on Friday?
   A Trainer Willinger   B Coach Willinger   C Bus Willinger

5. Who has to bring uniforms to the big match?
   A The school marching band   B The football team   C The cheerleaders

82

3 TEST Texte verstehen

6. The school says thank you to all the parents who ...
   A organized the food and drinks for the game.
   B gave money for the food and drinks for the game.
   C volunteered to drive the teenagers to the game.

7. In the high school competition the school's team ...
   A has won the semi-finals of the school's state.
   B has won the finals of the school's state.
   C has won the semi-finals of the whole country.

8. The school magazine 'The Humbler' ...
   A costs three dollars. One dollar goes to charity.
   B costs two dollars. One dollar fifty goes to charity.
   C costs two dollars. One dollar goes to charity.

You get one point for each correct answer.   Your points: /8

Conversations in the school dining room   Track 17

It's the Monday after a football match at an English school.
In the lunch break, some students are talking about the school's football match against a school from the next town. Other students are talking about how their school did in the big knowledge quiz.

3 Listen to the conversations and match the sentence halves.

1. Jim Harrison is ...
2. He broke his ankle ...
3. The accident happened because ...
4. Without their winger ...
5. In the end Bristol School ...
6. One of the boys complaining about the result ...
7. One of the members of the Nottingham Grammar knowledge team ...
8. Brian tells the story of his success ...
9. The names of the other team members in the challenge ...
10. Sarah is very good at ...
11. Luke is a specialist on ...
12. The subject that no member of the team ...
13. Brian says he could only answer the final question because ....
14. The final question was about the behaviour of apes ...

83

3 TEST Texte verstehen

A ... was a good-looking tall, dark-haired boy.
B ... Jim tripped up sprinting round a player from the opposite team.
C ... was really good at is biology.
D ... answering questions about politics.
E ... won the game comfortably.
F ... a winger on the school's football team.
G ... in threatening situations.
H ... to two girls.
I ... his biology teacher had taught them all about apes.
J ... the school team was unable to play effectively.
K ... questions from the world of sports.
L ... is no good at football.
M ... are Sarah and Luke.
N ... during the game.

You get one point for each correct answer.   Your points: /14

4 Read the following statements.

Some of them contain a mistake. Correct the false statements. Listen to the conversations again to check your corrections.

1. A boy says that he had expected the game to be a disaster.

2. He says that the team was incapable rather than unlucky.

3. The second boy tells the other boy not to be unfair. He claims that Jim hurt himself on purpose.

4. The two boys agree that the whole team is not very good.

5. The first boy believes that Jim will not be well again after the summer.

3 TEST   Texte verstehen

6. A girl says about her friend that she is interested in one of the boys from Nottingham Grammar.

7. The girl wants to know what happened when both teams had the same number of points and there was only one final question left.

8. Brian tells the girls that his team was rather relaxed in that situation because they knew they would win.

9. Brian says Sarah is a specialist on sports and Luke is good at questions about politics.

10. Brian describes how he first had to listen to the end of the question to make sure that he would give the correct answer.

You get one point for each correct answer.   **Your points: /10**

Your total points out of 40 points:

▶ More than 34? Very good.
▶ More than 30? Good.
▶ Less than 20? Have a look at the pages in this chapter again. You CAN do better.

4 Texte schreiben

Das solltest du am Ende der Klasse 8 können:

▷ Zusammenhängende, komplexere Texte zu vertrauten Themen, Briefe und Tagebucheinträge verfassen
▷ Bildvorgaben oder Absichten versprachlichen
▷ Durch das Entwickeln von Fragen Informationen ermitteln
▷ Längere Texte zusammenfassen, nacherzählen, fortführen, ergänzen oder Alternativen zu einem Text schriftlich darstellen

4.1 Mit vorgegebenen Informationen Texte erstellen

GOOD TO KNOW *Guided writing*

▶ Vorgegebene Informationen sollen dir dabei helfen, deinen Text inhaltlich zu strukturieren und zu gliedern. Sie geben dir erste Anhaltspunkte darüber, wovon dein Text handeln soll. Verwende **alle** Informationen. Du kannst jederzeit Dinge hinzufügen, sofern sie deinen Text sinnvoll ergänzen.
▶ Wenn du anhand von vorgegebenen Informationen Texte erstellst, solltest du stets **Adjektive** ergänzen, um deinen Text interessanter und lebendiger zu machen. Achte auch auf die richtige Satzstellung.
▶ Beschreibe, was die Personen deiner Geschichte sehen, hören oder riechen können. So kann sich der Leser deiner Geschichte besser in die Handlung hineinversetzen. Dies gilt gleichermaßen für beschreibende Texte, z. B. Texte in einer Werbebroschüre. Der Leser soll sich mithilfe deiner Informationen vor seinem inneren Auge ein Bild von der Umgebung oder der Situation machen können.

1 Compare the two texts below. Which text do you think is better? Why?

1. The town looks old and usually there are not many people around.

2. The little town seems like a ghost-town out of an old cowboy film. The buildings, with their broken windows, peeling paint and old-fashioned design, look as if no one has lived in them for ages. A warm wind is blowing through the streets, sometimes moving open doors and shutters with a rhythmic bang. It is the only sound to be heard in this deserted place where no one ever seems to set foot.

4.1 Mit vorgegebenen Informationen Texte erstellen

2 Net diagram: Native Americans

You want to write a text about present-day Native Americans for a school project. You can find information on the Internet and you can also look at the text on page 45 again. Before you start you need to structure your ideas.
Use the notes below to complete the net diagram. The main topics are given to you. Match the keywords with the topics.

*all over the USA   –   Mother Earth sacred   –   drug problems   –
peaceful, small communities   –   nobody's property   –   unemployment   –
nature-based religion   –   created by European settlers   –   50 % on reservations   –
infertile (= unfruchtbar) land   –   rest in villages, big cities   –
many tribes and languages   –   poor living conditions   –   about two million*

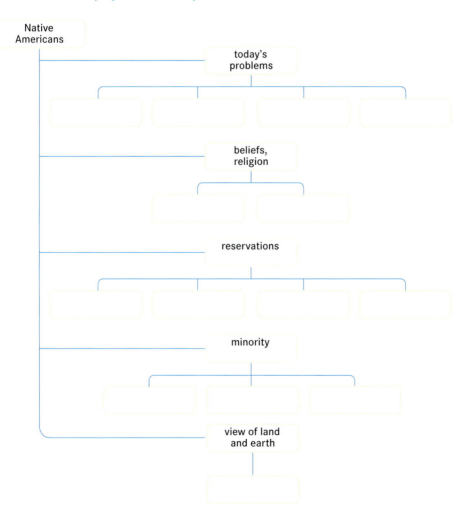

87

4 Texte schreiben

GOOD TO KNOW — Before writing the text

Wenn du einen Text schreibst, solltest du folgende Fragen bedenken:
- **WHO** am I writing this text for? → reader
- **WHY** am I writing this text? → purpose, intention
- **WHAT** do I want to say? → content
- **HOW** do I have to write the text? → style, language, layout

Die oben genannten Aspekte sind wichtig, da der Inhalt, die Sprache und manchmal sogar das Layout an deine(n) Leser und deine Absicht angepasst werden müssen. So macht es z. B. einen großen Unterschied, ob du eine Werbebroschüre für ein Produkt schreibst, das du verkaufen willst, oder einen nüchternen und ehrlichen Bericht über das Produkt.

Writing a draft
Der nächste wichtige Schritt besteht darin, einen Entwurf (= *draft*) zu schreiben. Verwende deine Notizen und die Gliederung als Hilfestellung.
Wieder musst du einige wichtige Aspekte berücksichtigen:

structure – style – language – intention

- Lass beim Schreiben immer einen breiten Rand für Korrekturen oder Ergänzungen.
- Benutze deine **Notizen** und deine **Gliederung** (*net diagram*) als Richtlinie.
- Versuche die Aufmerksamkeit des Lesers durch eine lebendige Einleitung zu gewinnen.
- Teile deinen Text in einzelne **Abschnitte** (*paragraphs*). Für jeden neuen Punkt deiner Gliederung beginnst du einen neuen Abschnitt. So kann sich der Leser schnell in deinem Text zurechtfinden.
- Ein gut strukturierter Text besteht immer aus drei Teilen: **Einleitung** (*introduction*), **Hauptteil** (*main part*) mit den einzelnen inhaltlich gegliederten Abschnitten und **Schluss** (*conclusion*).
- Beende deinen Text mit einem starken **Argument** bzw. einem aussagekräftigen, zusammenfassenden Schlusssatz. Dieser kann auch deine **eigene Meinung** enthalten.

3 Native Americans today – first draft

Write your first draft about Native Americans today. Use the net diagram and the guideline above for help.
You could start like this:
The sun is rising above the land. The prairie stretches out under the golden light, somewhere horses are grazing. Children start playing in the sun, smoke comes out of

4.1 Mit vorgegebenen Informationen Texte erstellen

the tepees and the men are preparing for the buffalo hunt.
This is the sort of scene you might imagine when thinking about Native Americans – or Indians, as they are called in cowboy films. But those times are gone. Present-day Native American reality has nothing to do with these old clichés anymore. …

GOOD TO KNOW — Improving your text

Wenn dein erster Entwurf fertig ist, solltest du den Inhalt und die Unterteilung in Abschnitte überprüfen:
▶ Hast du alle wichtigen Ideen berücksichtigt?
▶ Gibt es Formulierungen, die verbessert werden sollten?
▶ Sind die Abschnitte in einer sinnvollen Reihenfolge angeordnet?
▶ Gibt es Grammatik- oder Rechtschreibfehler?
▶ Sind die Sätze mit passenden Wörtern verbunden?

Tipp: Wenn du dir bei Grammatik oder Rechtschreibung unsicher bist, schreibe deinen Text auf dem Computer und überprüfe ihn mithilfe eines Rechtschreibprogramms.

Connectives

Connectives sind Bindewörter wie Konjunktionen, Wörter der Zeitenfolge und andere Begriffe, mit deren Hilfe du Satzteile aneinanderfügen kannst, damit eine sinnvolle Verbindung zwischen einzelnen Sätzen und Abschnitten entsteht.
In der nachfolgenden Übersicht findest du einige dieser hilfreichen Wörter.

Gedanken hinzufügen	
also	auch, ferner, ebenfalls
as well as	(sowohl) als auch, ebenso (wie)
indeed	in der Tat, tatsächlich, wirklich
in addition to	zusätzlich zu
furthermore	ferner, überdies, außerdem
moreover	weiter, überdies, außerdem, ferner
similarly	ähnlich, entsprechend
besides	sonst, noch dazu, überdies
what is more	noch dazu, was noch dazu kommt, außerdem
it must also be said that …	es muss noch gesagt werden, dass …
and we must not forget …	und man sollte nicht vergessen …
I would like to add …	Ich würde noch gerne hinzufügen …
another argument is …	ein weiteres Argument ist …

4 Texte schreiben

Aufzählungen und Reihenfolge

another point that should be mentioned is ...	ein anderer Punkt, der noch erwähnt werden sollte, ist ...
first(ly) ... next/secondly	erst(ens) ... danach/zweitens
to begin with	um anzufangen, zunächst
on second thoughts	nach reiflicher Überlegung, wenn ich es mir recht überlege
above all	vor allem
on top of (that)	darüber hinaus
then	dann
finally	schließlich, letztendlich
in conclusion	zum Schluss, schließlich, zusammenfassend
finally	abschließend, am Ende

Vergleiche anstellen

compared with	verglichen mit
in comparison with	im Vergleich zu/mit
likewise	ebenfalls, gleichfalls, desgleichen, ebenso
equally	ebenso, gleich(ermaßen), in gleicher Weise
whereas the former ...	während/wohingegen der erste ...
... the latter	(macht) der letzte(re) ...
as ... as	so ... wie

sich auf etwas beziehen

with reference to	bezüglich
referring to	mit Verweis auf, sich auf etwas/ jemanden beziehend
with regard to	hinsichtlich, bezüglich, was ... betrifft
the former says ...	der Vorherige/Erstgenannte sagt ...

4.1 Mit vorgegebenen Informationen Texte erstellen

einen Standpunkt relativieren bzw. von einem anderen abheben	
however	wie auch immer, jedoch
but of course	aber/jedoch natürlich
on the one hand ...	auf der einen Seite ...
... on the other hand	andererseits, auf der anderen Seite
on the contrary/in contrast	im Gegenteil/im Gegensatz zu
despite	trotz, ungeachtet
nonetheless	nichtsdestoweniger, dennoch
instead of	anstatt, anstelle von
yet	dennoch, trotzdem, jedoch
apart from/except for	mit Ausnahme von, abgesehen von
in spite of the fact	ungeachtet der Tatsache, trotz
otherwise	sonst, andernfalls, im Übrigen

etwas umformulieren	
in other words	mit anderen Worten
that means/that is to say	das heißt so viel wie, was bedeutet
a better way of putting it is	um es anders/besser zu sagen
to put it more simply	um es einfacher zu sagen, um es genauer zu sagen
to put it differently	mit anderen Worten, um es anders zu sagen

Gedankengang abschließen, Resümee ziehen	
consequently	folglich, deshalb, als Folge
thus	so, folgendermaßen, folglich, demgemäß
as a result	die Folge ist / war, folglich
for that reason	aus diesem Grund
accordingly	folglich, entsprechend
it follows that	daraus folgt, dass ...
therefore	folglich, deshalb, deswegen
to conclude/in conclusion	um es abzuschließen, abschließend
all in all	alles in allem
in brief	in Kürze
on the whole	im Großen und Ganzen
to sum up	um es zusammenzufassen

4 Texte schreiben

4 Find suitable connectives.

Translate these sentences. Some parts have already been translated for you. Use suitable connectives from the lists above. Sometimes several different connectives are possible.

1. In der Tat leiden die Indianer heute oft unter schlechten Lebensbedingungen.
   _____ Native Americans today often suffer from poor living conditions.

2. Was noch dazu kommt ist, dass sie oft Probleme mit Alkohol haben.
   _____
   _____

3. Einerseits kommen diese Probleme aus der Zeit der frühen europäischen Siedler, andererseits müssen sie wirklich selbst etwas tun, um ihre Situation zu verbessern.
   _____ date back to the time of the early European settlers; _____
   _____ really need to do something themselves to improve their situation.

4. Verglichen mit der Situation anderer Minderheiten in den USA sind die Indianer hinsichtlich der Arbeitsbedingungen immer noch benachteiligt.
   _____ other minorities in the USA, Native Americans are, _____
   _____ working conditions, still underprivileged.

5. Dennoch sind einige Indianer sehr erfolgreich in ihrem Job.
   _____
   _____

6. Folglich versuchen immer mehr Indianer diesen Beispielen zu folgen.
   _____ more and more
   _____.

7. Obwohl viele Amerikaner die Kultur der Indianer immer noch nicht verstehen, verdienen einige Indianer ihren Unterhalt mit dem Tourismus.
   _____ still do not understand Native American culture
   _____ earn their living with tourism.

8. Überdies hat sich der Verkauf von indianischem Schmuck in den letzten Jahren als wahre Goldgrube entpuppt.
   _____, the selling of Native American jewelry has turned out to be a real money-spinner in recent years.

4.2 Eine Reisebroschüre erstellen

> **GOOD TO KNOW** — Tipps zum Schreiben einer Broschüre

Wenn man eine Broschüre über einen Urlaubsort erstellt, muss man folgende Punkte beachten:
- Die Texte dürfen nicht zu lang sein. Sie sollen aber so interessant geschrieben sein, dass das Interesse des Lesers geweckt wird, diesen Ort zu besuchen.
- Der Leser soll Informationen über den Ort erhalten, z. B. über dessen Geschichte, sehenswerte Plätze, Freizeitangebot und Unterbringungsmöglichkeiten.
- Es sollten Hinweise gegeben werden, wo der Leser weitere Informationen erhalten kann, z. B. eine Internetadresse oder die Anschrift einer Touristeninformation.
- Um die Broschüre optisch ansprechend zu gestalten, können Fotos oder Landkarten hinzugefügt werden.
- Damit der Leser schnell die Informationen finden kann, nach denen er sucht, sollte die Broschüre nach Unterthemen geordnet sein (z. B. Geschichte, Sehenswürdigkeiten, Einkaufen, Essen und Trinken, Freizeit, Unterbringung).

1 Bryce Canyon National Park

Write the text for a brochure about Bryce Canyon National Park. Use the information given below. Remember to order the information.

- not a real canyon, part of the Pink Cliffs → stone pillars (= Steinsäulen), arches (=Bögen) and rock pinnacles (=Felsnadeln), were carved out of the Paunsaugunt Plateau by rain, wind, ice and snow over millions of years; 146 sq km
- appear in different colors depending on the incidence of light (= Lichteinfall)
- 60 million years ago sea covered southwest Utah; deposits (= Ablagerungen) of lime (= Kalk), sand and mud were pressed to stone under the weight of water
- 13 million years ago: massive tectonic movement (= Bewegungen der Erdkruste) put land into slant (= Schräglage); water ran off (= abfließen)
- erosion formed rugged (= zerklüftet) stone formation of Bryce Canyon
- was declared nature reserve in 1928; named after Mormon settler Ebenezer Bryce; original name (given by Paiute): Unka-tim-pewa-wince-pock-ich (meaning: red rocks like standing men in a valley)
- Visitor Center near "Fairyland View" (entrance to National Park) → information on Bryce Canyon National Park; slide show (= Diashow), exhibitions (= Ausstellungen)

4 Texte schreiben

- along road through National Park: eleven spectacular lookout points (= Aussichtspunkte), about 2500 meters high → amazing view over rock formations
- 100 km well-developed hiking trail network (= Wanderwege-Netz)
- highest point: 'Rainbow Point' (2776 m)
- amphitheater of sandstone belongs to most impressive spectacles of nature
- Navajo Loop Trail: from "Sunrise Point" through rock pinnacles of "Queen's Garden" and back; 2.5 km long; difference in meters of height of walk: 100 m
- guided tours on horseback, starting near Bryce Canyon Lodge
- helicopter flights above Bryce Canyon, starting at Ruby's Inn; about $55 per person

- Hotels:
- Best Western Ruby's Inn → big hotel (370 rooms) shortly before entrance to National Park; restaurants, souvenir shop, rodeo (summer only), pool, campground (Address: Utah Hwy. 63, Bryce, UT 84764, phone: 435/834-5341); price category: middle

- Bryce Canyon Lodge → only accommodation inside National Park; about 80 years old hotel made of massive logs (= Baumstämme); 114 rooms en suite (= mit Bad) plus 40 log cabins (= Blockhütten); reservation has to be made at least eight months in advance (phone: 435/834-5361); price category: middle

- Pink Cliffs Bryce Village → simple hostel (= Herberge), about 5 km from entrance to National Park, 68 rooms (phone: 435/834-5303); price category: lower – middle
- Camping: North Campground close to Visitor Center / Sunset Campground (4 km away from Visitor Centre) / big campground at Ruby's Inn
- Information: Bryce Canyon National Park, UT 84717, phone: 435/834-5322
- Entrance fee (=Eintrittspreis): seven days pass per car: $10
- seven days pass for one person with bike: $3.

4.3 Briefe verfassen

> **GOOD TO KNOW** — *Informal and formal letters*
>
> Ein Brief besteht immer aus **Anrede**, **Text**, **Schluss** und **Grußworten** mit deiner **Unterschrift**. Formelle Briefe unterscheiden sich von Briefen an Freunde und Familie.
>
> Wenn du einen englischen Brief schreibst, musst du dir erst überlegen, ob er für einen Freund beziehungsweise ein Mitglied deiner Familie gedacht ist oder an eine Person oder Organisation geschickt werden soll, die du noch nicht kennst. Solche Briefe schreibt man, um nach Informationen zu fragen, sich zu beschweren, sich um einen Job oder Ähnliches zu bewerben oder jemandem seine Meinung mitzuteilen (z. B. in einem Leserbrief an eine Zeitung).
>
> Beide Briefarten haben im Prinzip den gleichen Aufbau. Zuerst kommt die Anrede, in der du den Namen des Adressaten nennst, dann kommt dein Text und am Schluss nette Grußworte und deine Unterschrift.
>
> Je nachdem, an wen der Brief geht, müssen Anrede, Grußworte sowie der Inhalt des Briefes angepasst werden.
>
> *Informal letters* – **Briefe an Familie, Freunde und gute Bekannte**
> ▶ Die Anrede ist persönlich, z. B. Dear Sarah. Nach der Anrede steht ein Komma und du schreibst in der nächsten Zeile groß weiter (anders als im Deutschen!).
> ▶ In deinem Text darfst du umgangssprachliche Begriffe sowie Kurzformen (I'm) und unkomplizierte, kurze Sätze verwenden.
> ▶ Zum Schluss verwendest du herzliche Grußworte, je nachdem, wie gut du den Adressaten kennst. Vergiss das Komma nach dem Grußwort nicht (!) und unterschreibe mit deinem Vornamen.
>
> *Formal letters* – **Briefe an unbekannte Personen oder Organisationen**
> Denk zuerst darüber nach, was du alles in dem Brief schreiben möchtest und überlege dir eine gute Reihenfolge, z. B. Anrede, Lob, der Grund für dein Schreiben, dein Text, höfliche Verabschiedung.
> ▶ Die Anrede sollte höflich sein. Kennst du den Namen der Person, verwende ihn in der Anrede (Dear Mrs Evans, …). Kennst du ihn nicht oder weißt nicht einmal, ob ein Mann oder eine Frau deinen Brief lesen wird, benutzt du eine allgemeine Anrede ohne Namen (Dear Sir or Madam, …).
> ▶ Bei deinem Text solltest du darauf achten, dass du die Langformen benutzt (I am), keine Umgangssprache oder unpassenden Wörter verwendest und höflich schreibst.
> ▶ Als Grußformel zum Schluss kannst du, unabhängig davon, ob du den Namen der Person kennst, Yours sincerely oder Yours truly schreiben (in Amerika ist letzteres üblicher).

4 Texte schreiben

EXAMPLE — *A formal letter*

Hanno Beckman
D-32051 Herford
05221-65826
H.Beckman@schoolweb.de

March 25, 2011

Hopi Cultural Centre and Tourist Information
P.O. Box 129
Hopi Reservation
Arizona, USA

Dear Sir or Madam,

I received your address from my English teacher, Mrs. Schulz. I am writing to you because our class is planning to visit the Hopi Reservation in October this year.
We have learned a lot about Native American culture and history at school.
That is why we have decided to visit a reservation during our exchange trip to the USA. I hope you will recommend some interesting places for us to visit.
Do you have a Visitor Center, museum or something similar?
We are especially interested in the living conditions and traditional housing and culture of Hopi Indians. A guided tour in English would be wonderful. We have had three years of English lessons so far, so hopefully we will be able to understand most of the tour. We would be very grateful if you could help us with information or leaflets, including details of accommodation for school groups at the Reservation.
If you need further information, you can also contact me by e-mail or telephone.
I am looking forward to hearing from you soon.

Yours truly,

Hanno Beckman

4.3 Briefe verfassen

GOOD TO KNOW	Nützliche Redewendungen für einen formellen Brief
Dear …, / Dear Sir or Madam, …	Sehr geehrte(r) …,
Dear Ladies and Gentlemen, …	Sehr geehrte Damen und Herren,
I am writing regarding …	Ich schreibe Ihnen bezüglich …
I am writing to ask for/about …	Ich schreibe um nach …zu fragen / bitten
With reference to / Further to your letter of …	Bezüglich Ihres Briefes vom … (Datum)
I would like to thank you for …	Ich würde Ihnen gerne für … danken.
Would you please be so kind as to …	Wären Sie bitte so nett … (zu tun)
Please accept my apologies for …	Bitte entschuldigen Sie mein …
Please send me …	Bitte senden Sie mir … zu.
Thank you for your time and attention.	Vielen Dank für Ihre Zeit und Mühe.
I am available for an interview …	Ich stehe Ihnen für ein Gespräch zur Verfügung …
… at your convenience.	… wann immer es Ihnen passt.
Enclosed please find …	Anbei (finden Sie) …
I have enclosed …	Ich habe … beigelegt.
Looking forward to meeting you soon.	Ich freue mich darauf, Sie bald zu treffen.
I am looking forward to hearing from you.	Ich würde mich über eine Antwort sehr freuen.
I would be happy to help in any way I can.	Ich würde mich freuen, Ihnen zu helfen, wenn ich kann.
Please feel free to contact me if you have any questions.	Bitte zögern Sie nicht mich zu kontaktieren, wenn Sie irgendwelche Fragen haben.
(Yours) sincerely/faithfully/truly …	Mit freundlichen Grüßen/ Hochachtungsvoll, Ihr(e)
Best regards, …	Mit freundlichen Grüßen, …

4 Texte schreiben

1 A letter to your host family

Imagine you are in Mrs. Schulz's English class. In a few weeks you will go on your exchange trip to the USA. You will stay with an American family, the Sandermans, while you are there. Mrs. Schulz has told you to write a letter to your host family to introduce yourself.

Write a formal letter using these notes:
- reason for writing: going to stay with them in October
- received their address from Mrs. Schulz
- thank them for letting you stay with them
- excited and looking forward to staying with them
- facts about yourself (age, where you come from, hobbies)
- enclosed: photograph of yourself
- facts about your family (brothers and sisters, mum and dad, pets, ...)
- planned program: school in the mornings, excursions in the afternoons → family only in the evenings and at the weekends
- what you don't eat: fish, hot tomatoes → tell in advance
- apology for possible language mistakes in your letter
- hope to get an answer soon

2 The Sandermans' response

A few days after you sent your letter to the Sandermans you receive an e-mail from the family. Unfortunately something went wrong and the sentences have been jumbled. Bring them into the correct order.

Dear ... [your name],

1. *for   Thank   friendly   you   letter.   your*

2. *very excited   before.   never had   We are also   because   we have   a   German pupil   our house   in   about your stay*

3. *well.   about yourself   each other   Now that   we are sure   so many things   you have told us   get on with   that we will*

4. *a very nice person   You seem   many things   to be   and   in common.   we have*

5. *some things   tell   about us.   you   Let us*

6. *five people: mother Caroline,   consists of   daughter Jules.   and   Our family   Grandpa Jimmy,   son Danny   father Dan,*

4.3 Briefe verfassen

7. you can   in this country.   all of us   as is usual   Of course
   our first names,   call   by

8. too;   we've got a dog,   his name is   terrier
   Oh, and   and   Brutus.   he's a Yorkshire

9. to school   Danny   you can go   with him.
   years old,   is   so   nearly fifteen

10. It is funny,   so I guess   but you have   you will be good friends
    nearly the same hobbies,   in no time.

11. him better.   Please   and Danny   as soon as possible
    the next e-mail,   so that you   write back   will answer   can get to know

12. soon.   looking forward   to meeting you   We are

    Yours,
    Caroline, Dan, Jimmy, Danny and Jules.

3 A letter from the exchange trip organisation

Mrs. Schulz has organised the exchange trip with the help of a professional organisation. They have sent you a letter but the person who wrote it does not know what a formal letter should look like.
Turn this informal letter into a formal one.

> Hello Hanno Beckman!
>
> thank you for going abroad with the Europe-America Student Exchange.
> We just want to let you know that everything has been organized for your trip.
> Look into the envelope and you will find the tickets for your flight.
> If you have any questions or problems before you leave for America, please
> call our office whenever you have the time and want to.
> Since it is my job to help, I will have to do it if I can.
>
> Lots of greetings,
>
> Billy Backins, Europe-America Student Exchange

4 Texte schreiben

4.4 Geschichten zu Bildern schreiben

REMEMBER *Free text composition*

Fotos sind ein guter Ausgangspunkt zum Schreiben von Geschichten. Sie geben dir lediglich einen Hinweis darauf, was vielleicht passiert sein könnte, legen dich aber nicht fest, sodass du deine Geschichte frei entwickeln kannst.
Folgende Entscheidungen musst du treffen:
- ▶ Welche Textart möchte ich wählen?
- ▶ Wie und wer sollen die Charaktere sein?
- ▶ Wie soll die Handlung verlaufen?

Wenn du eine Geschichte zu einem Foto schreiben möchtest, solltest du dir zunächst das **Foto** sehr **genau ansehen** und dir eine passende Geschichte dazu überlegen. Sieht man Personen, solltest du überlegen, wie diese sich wohl gerade fühlen oder wie die Beziehungen der Personen untereinander sind. Mach dir auf einem Blatt erste **Notizen**, damit du beim Schreiben nichts vergisst. Sammle so viele Gedanken wie möglich, du kannst sie später ja auch wieder verwerfen.

Nun musst du dich entscheiden, welche Art von Text du zu dem Foto schreiben willst. Es gibt viele verschiedene Möglichkeiten. Jede Textsorte hat bestimmte Inhalte und Eigenschaften, die du beim Schreiben beachten solltest.

Hier findest du eine Liste von Testsorten und ihren wichtigsten Merkmalen:

Newspaper report
headline, passive forms, description without feelings, quotations, formal style

Advertisement
name of product, adjectives, description how to use product, short text

Personal profile
family background, character, personal information about the relations between the people, informal style

Diary entry
written from one perspective only, thoughts and feelings, no direct speech

Scene from a play
includes stage directions (= Regieanweisungen), different characters, usually just one setting and time, no big jumps in the plot

Short Story
no introduction, usually no shift of place and time, climax has to be reached quickly, only a few characters and simple storyline

4.4 Geschichten zu Bildern schreiben

> **EXAMPLE** — Fotogeschichten spannend erzählen
>
> Um deine Geschichte besonders **spannend** zu gestalten, kannst du bei fast allen Textsorten **wörtliche Rede** einbauen. Auf diese Weise kannst du deine Leser an den Gedanken deiner Figuren teilhaben lassen. Verwende auf jeden Fall **Adjektive**. Wirklich packend werden Fotogeschichten, wenn sie ein überraschendes Ende haben.
> Lies dazu folgendes Beispiel:
>
> Boring, boring, boring.
> That was what Kalli thought when his parents told him that he was to spend his autumn holidays with his aunt and uncle in Scotland.
> He didn't even know these people very well. All he knew was that they were really old and lived in an ancient castle somewhere in the Highlands.
> Have you ever been to Scotland in autumn? There are some sunny days, all right, but most of the time it is cold, foggy and wet. There is not much to do in the lonely old villages up in the Highlands. Only old people around. Kalli remembered the one summer that he had spent in the Highlands with his parents. He had been allowed to bring a friend, they had stayed in a big hotel and the boys had been outside all day long, riding their bikes and playing in the fields.
> But this was different.
> When he arrived, the castle did not look very inviting. It was drizzling and the old walls smelt of cold, wet stone. Inside it wasn't much better. There were only small windows and since it was nearly dark outside, hardly any light came through the windows.
> Aunt Mary showed Kalli his room and lit the lights. Now that it was bright, the only thing he could see was grey stones. No tapestry or colour inside his room. The walls looked just as they did from the outside of the castle. 'Great,' Kalli sighed. 'I'm really looking forward to three weeks in this old bunker.'
> After dinner Kalli was sitting in the main hall with his Uncle Andy and Aunt Mary. Here, near the open fireplace, it was almost cosy. "Did your mum and dad tell you we have a ghost here?" Uncle Andy asked. Oh, no – not that! A ghost? How old did he think Kalli was? Only little children and fools believed in ghosts!
> "I know, nearly every old Scottish castle has a ghost, but ours is a special one," Uncle Andy went on. And then he told Kalli the story of a Spanish tourist who had visited the castle just before the First World War. Accidentally he had been locked in when the castle was closed for visitors in the evening. "He had tried to get out, but the gates are made of iron and there is no escape without a key!" Uncle Andy went on. Kalli was not interested in the story at all, so he murmured, "Let me guess, he didn't get out alive and now his ghost haunts everyone who runs around the castle with a key?"

4 Texte schreiben

"No, they rescued him the next day. But Carlos, that's his name, liked the castle so much that when he was killed in World War One, his ghost returned to the peace and quiet of this old castle." Now that was a different ghost story for once, Kalli thought. But the next moment he had to smile. Must have been a stupid person if he volunteered to spend his nights haunting this boring, deserted place. "So, what does he do?" Kalli asked. "Lock himself in every night, howling and crying?" "You'll find out for yourself," Uncle Andy said with a mysterious look on his face.

Four days later Kalli's aunt and uncle had to go to a birthday party. He could have gone with them, but the last thing he needed was more old people. Though he had to admit that Uncle Andy and Aunt Mary were not so bad after all. They wanted to stay over night and had left him enough food and some DVDs, so that he wouldn't get bored. In the early evening Kalli decided to go for a walk before the sun went down. It was foggy again but somehow he had learned to enjoy the quiet of the surroundings. The fog made the place look even more mysterious and Kalli liked to imagine how it might have been to live here at the time of the Scottish clans.

He had nearly reached the castle again when he suddenly noticed that something was wrong. It took him several seconds to realize what made him feel so strange. A sudden terror befell him. He had forgotten to take his keys. Just as Aunt Mary had told him he had closed the big, wooden door and heavy iron gate of the castle behind him when he had left an hour ago. But without his keys there would be no way of opening them again.

Just thinking of a cold night outside the castle made him shiver. Or was it the wind? Kalli looked around him. It was completely calm, but even though there was no movement to be seen in the trees, a cold breeze touched his face. He looked around and suddenly heard a strange sound. "I'm going mad!" he said out loud, without having wanted to speak. "The gate, the gate ..." the wind seemed to say.

Kalli ran towards the gate in despair and guess what he found? He was sure that he had closed the gate, but now it swung open in the non-existing wind just in front of him.

Kalli went through and with a smile on his face he murmured: "Thank you, Carlos!"

4.4 Geschichten zu Bildern schreiben

1 **Changing the perspective**

Rewrite the story from Kalli's perspective. Imagine you are Kalli and you are writing a letter to your parents in which you explain to them what happened.

2 **An advertisement**

Use the picture on the right to write an advertisement for one of the following products:

A: Adventure holidays
B: A new car
C: A life insurance

Remember that your slogan should be short but strong!

GOOD TO KNOW	*Checklist: How to write your text*

- ✔ Entscheide, was für einen Text du schreiben möchtest.
- ✔ Sammle Ideen und Wörter, die du verwenden könntest.
- ✔ Ordne deine Ideen und plane deinen Text. Eine Mindmap oder eine Liste von Argumenten können hilfreich sein.
- ✔ Schreibe mithilfe deiner Notizen einen ersten Entwurf.
- ✔ Überprüfe deinen Text. Enthält er alle wichtigen Teile? Passt der Stil zur Textsorte? Ist der Text interessant?
- ✔ Überprüfe die Rechtschreibung und Grammatik auf Fehler. Denk daran, dass du deinen Computer oder ein Wörterbuch zu Hilfe nehmen kannst.

3 **Right time, right place**

Finish writing the story about a car accident.

It was Saturday morning and Laurel was on his way home. He worked night shifts as a doctor in the local hospital. After fourteen hours of work he was tired and just wanted to lie down and sleep.

As usual he had to drive more than half an hour to reach home. He lived in the Native American reservation in Kayenta, close to the famous Monument Valley where all the old Western movies had been filmed. Laurel belonged to the tribe of the Navajo and even

4 Texte schreiben

though he had lived in Chicago for some time to study medicine, he had never wanted to live anywhere else than here, close to the Grand Canyon. The land was dry and the summers were hotter than anyone could imagine, but he loved his home: the red sand, the bizarre rock formations and in between the Hogans. Of course, these round houses made of clay and wood were more of a tourist attraction than a real home these days, but Laurel and his family still lived in them during the summer, because inside they were much cooler than modern houses.

He was just thinking of how his grandmother had used to wait for him in front of their Hogan when he came home from school, when suddenly he was brought back into reality. There was a man standing on the road, waving at him with a big, red stop sign. A bit further down the road …

4 A newspaper report

Here are some pictures. This time you have to write a short newspaper report. Include some advice and rules of behaviour in your article.

You can either describe what happened in a special incident or speak more generally about children riding their bikes on the street.

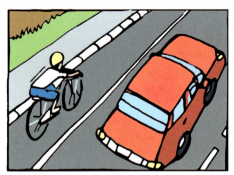

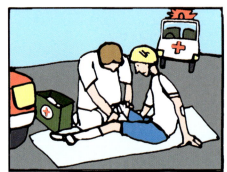

4.4 Geschichten zu Bildern schreiben

| GOOD TO KNOW | Arbeit mit einem einsprachigen Wörterbuch |

Wenn du ein Wort nicht kennst, benutzt du normalerweise ein zweisprachiges Wörterbuch, also Deutsch-Englisch oder Englisch-Deutsch.
Wenn du aber englische Texte schreiben willst, wirst du feststellen, dass ein **einsprachiges Wörterbuch** (Englisch-Englisch) oft sehr hilfreich sein kann, denn hier findest du zusätzliche Informationen, die dir dabei helfen, die englischen Wörter richtig zu verwenden.

- ▶ **Wortart** Ist das Wort ein Nomen (*n*), ein Adjektiv (*adj*) oder ein Adverb (*adv*)? Gibt es das Wort auch als Verb (*v*)? Eine Liste der Abkürzungen findest du meist vorn im Wörterbuch.
- ▶ **Eigenschaft** Bei einem Verb erfährst du, ob es regelmäßig oder unregelmäßig ist und mit welchen Präpositionen es verwendet wird.
- ▶ **Verwendung** Ist das Wort umgangssprachlich oder kann man es auch für sachliche und formelle Texte verwenden?
- ▶ **Bedeutung** Manche Wörter haben verschiedene Bedeutungen und passen nicht in jedem Zusammenhang. Das Wörterbuch zeigt dir in diesem Fall auch andere Wörter, die in einem bestimmten Zusammenhang besser passen könnten.
- ▶ **Wendungen** Typische feststehende Redewendungen machen deinen Text interessant und lassen ihn professionell wirken. Du findest sie, wenn du ein bestimmtes Wort nachschlägst, das in der Redewendung vorkommt.
- ▶ **Beziehungen** Wörter aus der gleichen Wortfamilie und Wörter mit gleicher oder gegensätzlicher Bedeutung machen deinen Text abwechslungsreich. Zudem erweiterst du deinen Wortschatz, wenn du nicht immer die gleichen Wörter verwendest.

5 An adventure story

Use this picture to write a short adventure story.
An adventure story is a story, in which something unexpected happens (= Abenteuergeschichte). You can make it more interesting by describing feelings, the surroundings or what people see, smell and hear. Use adjectives and direct speech.

4 Texte schreiben

4.5 Zeitungsartikel schreiben

REMEMBER — **Merkmale und Aufbau eines Zeitungsartikels**

Zeitungsartikel informieren den Leser über ein Thema oder eine Geschichte. Sie sind in korrekter, klarer Sprache geschrieben (keine Umgangssprache!) und geben Antworten auf (fast) alle der wichtigen Fragen.

Die sechs wichtigsten Fragen, die ein Zeitungsbericht beantworten sollte, sind:
- Who?   →   Wer?
- What?   →   Was?
- Where?   →   Wo?
- When?   →   Wann?
- Why?   →   Warum?
- How?   →   Wie?

Structure of newspaper articles

Headline (=Schlagzeile)

Function	catches the reader's attention
Style	uses simple tenses and sometimes idioms (= Redewendungen) and 'flashy' (= auffällig) vocabulary or puns (= Wortspiele)

Introductory sentence (= Einleitungssatz)

Function	gives a general overview
Style	often uses the present perfect tense

Main body (= Text)

Function	describes who did what, when, where, and sometime why and how
Style	starts with the most important paragraphs, as readers often do not finish reading an article presents quotes (=Zitate) from the people involved may be factual or may include a clear interpretation or opinion (depending on the kind of newspaper)

4.5 Zeitungsartikel schreiben

1 A clever idea
Read this newspaper article about the clever idea of a teenager. Look closely at the tenses that are used. Underline some examples of the different tenses you find and say why they are used.

Teenager Uses Brains and Old Football Shirt and Ends Up with Car

San Diego, CA
15-year-old Ben Rosenbaum swapped his own photo for a car on the Internet

"My grandfather in Germany told me about this German guy who offered an autograph card of a famous football star on the Internet and swapped it for a biro," explains Ben Rosenbaum. Indeed, the "German guy" became quite well known in his own country and was even invited to talk shows. He had swapped every item he got
5   for another one, the items becoming more and more valuable. The idea behind the action was that the young man wanted to have a car but didn't have the money to buy one. However, six months after he had started with the autograph card he had an old but efficiently working car.
"I thought, why not do the same?" says Ben. "The only problem was that I did not
10 have an autograph card or any other item that people would like to swap something valuable for." But then the clever boy had a good idea. He put on an old football shirt that his grandfather had once given him for his birthday, had a picture of himself in the shirt taken and signed it. "It does not matter who is on the card, really," Ben explains. "As long as people think it might be a famous person, they want to have it.
15 So I was hoping for even better things to come."
The "autograph card" was swapped for a mug. The mug was swapped for a book, the book for a game of cards, the game of cards for a football and so on and so on. Twenty-one items later the postman brought Ben a coffee machine and a few items later he was the proud owner of a mountain bike.
20 "One person even offered me his wife as a cook for one evening. He really wanted that bike. But I thought you can't swap another guy's wife, so I turned the offer down."
Ben is now the proud owner of an old Mercedes. When asked why he does not go on swapping he explains that the car is all he ever wanted. "Besides, you should not
25 forget how much work swapping on the Internet can be. You have to compare offers and upload pictures of your items. Once the items became too big for the postman I had to arrange meeting points and dates for handing them over," the teenager adds. After his surprising success some of his friends tried their luck as well, but were not as successful as Ben. "I guess people think it's fun when they see it for the first time,
30 but after a while they get bored and suspicious," is Ben's explanation for his friends' failure. Ben himself developed into a local hero. After he had published his success on his website, starting with the coffee machine, everyone could follow his swapping

4 Texte schreiben

actions on the web. The teenager was interviewed by the local radio station as well as three national and two international newspapers.

35 Even though he does not want to swap anymore, he is already involved in some Internet auctions of old toys and books he does not need.

"You can make money on the web easily. And I want a new radio for my car!", he grins.

2 Fill in this grid with information from the article.

Who?	
What?	
When?	
Where?	
Why?	
How?	

GOOD TO KNOW — Different kinds of newspapers

Da Zeitungsartikel objektiv über interessante Ereignisse informieren sollen, solltest du deine persönliche Meinung nicht in einem Bericht zum Ausdruck bringen. Manche Zeitungen oder Zeitschriften vermitteln aber eher Meinungen und Gefühle als Tatsachen. Es gibt zwei Arten von Zeitungen und Zeitschriften.
Hier findest du die wichtigsten Merkmale:

Serious newspapers (= ernsthafte Zeitungen)
- ▶ objektiv, Berichte über Fakten, Tatsachen
- ▶ formale Sprache
- ▶ komlexe Sätze und Wörter, die nicht aus der Umgangssprache stammen
- ▶ verschiedene Blickwinkel, geben unterschiedliche Meinungen wieder
- ▶ weniger Bilder, mehr Text
- → Die Leser werden auf neutrale Weise informiert und sollen sich selbst eine Meinung bilden.

Popular newspapers (*also called 'tabloids'* = Boulevardzeitungen)
- ▶ an Sensationen interessiert, sprechen Gefühle an
- ▶ schreiben über mögliche Gründe, ohne dass es Beweise gibt
- ▶ verwenden Umgangsprache
- ▶ kürzere Sätze und einfache Wörter
- ▶ wenig Text, viele farbige Bilder
- ▶ oft Berichte über Stars, Klatsch und Gerüchte
- → Die Leser werden unterhalten und informiert, Artikel bieten oft fertige Meinungen.

4.5 Zeitungsartikel schreiben

3 **The girl that wanted to live**
Read this newspaper article from a popular newspaper. Then rewrite the story to give it a happy ending.

Homeless Girl Found Dead under Bridge

Chicago, Illinois
A 13-year-old runaway was found frozen to death underneath a highway bridge yesterday morning.
Yesterday morning a street cleaner found the corpse of a young girl under a highway bridge in the suburbs of Chicago. The girl was lying on the ground, covered only with an old newspaper. The coroner says the girl froze to death during the night. She was probably surprised by the sudden onset of winter[1]. The police have talked to several teenagers that live on the street and knew the girl. "Our investigations have shown that the girl's name is Tammy D. She ran away from home five weeks ago after a terrible argument with her parents," says Police officer Stanley Morgan.
Another youngster living on the streets mentioned that Tammy had regretted having run away from home and had been thinking about going back. "She wanted to tell her parents that she was sorry, but she was not brave enough to go and talk to them. She was afraid they might be too angry about her running away. She feared that they would start arguing again and decided to let her parents know where she was. She phoned them and left a message on their answering machine. That was two days ago."
Unfortunately, the young girl died before her parents could find her and take her home. She will be buried in the graveyard of her hometown.

[1] Wintereinbruch

EXAMPLE

This is how your article could start:

Runaway Happily United with Parents after Argument

Chicago, Illinois
A 13 year-old runaway was found underneath a highway bridge and taken home by her parents yesterday morning.
Yesterday morning a sad story took a happy ending in the suburbs of Chicago.

4 TEST Texte schreiben

Test

1 Match the connectives with the German translation.

1.	What is more, …	A	bezüglich
2.	A better way of putting it is …	B	ebenfalls, gleichermaßen
3.	Likewise, …	C	deshalb, als Folge
4.	For that reason …	D	was noch dazu kommt, außerdem
5.	On the whole …	E	jedoch
6.	Indeed, …	F	im Großen und Ganzen
7.	Above all, …	G	darüber hinaus
8.	Furthermore, …	H	ungeachtet der Tatsache, trotz
9.	On second thoughts …	I	anstatt, anstelle von
10.	In spite of the fact …	J	ferner, überdies, außerdem
11.	Consequently, …	K	aus diesem Grund
12.	All in all, …	L	um es besser/genauer zu sagen
13.	In addition to …	M	ähnlich, entsprechend
14.	With reference to …	N	vor allem
15.	Similarly, …	O	zusätzlich zu
16.	On top of that …	P	schließlich
17.	Finally, …	Q	nach reiflicher Überlegung
18.	However, …	R	nichtsdestoweniger, dennoch
19.	Nevertheless, …	S	alles in allem
20.	Instead of …	T	in der Tat, tatsächlich

You get one point for each correct answer.   **Your points:** /20

2 Translate the following sentences into German.

1. Please accept my apologies for my late reply.
2. I would be happy to help in any way I can.
3. I am available for an interview at your convenience.
4. I am writing regarding your job offer from Sunday's paper.
5. Please feel free to contact me if you have any questions.
6. Thank you for your time and attention.
7. Enclosed you will find my photograph and address.
8. I am looking forward to hearing from you.
9. I would like to thank you for your immediate answer.
10. Could you, please, give me some further information about the job?

You get two points for each correct answer.   **Your points:** /20

4 TEST Texte schreiben

3 Read the following information on a German immigrant who arrived at Ellis Island in 1923 in order to start a better life in America.

Then write a letter to her parents in English, in which she describes her feelings after she has arrived at her new home. Consider the following ideas:
- Her family at home
- Her worries about the new job with the Stanfords
- The long journey by ship (three weeks) that lies behind her
- Her feelings when she saw the Statue of Liberty and New York Harbor
- Her anxiety about passing the medical examination on Ellis Island. (If an immigrant did not pass that examination, he or she was sent back home on the next ship.)
- Friends in the new country?
- The new language

name:	Martha Hüner
sex:	female
year of birth:	1901
town/country:	Seestemünde / Germany
port of departure:	Bremerhaven
type of ship:	steamship
destination:	USA
port of arrival:	New York
destination in new country:	New York City
profession in new country:	nanny (child carer)
marital status:	single
family members on journey:	none
address in new country:	
property:	one suitcase
language abilities:	German, little English
reason for migration:	looking for a better job in America
relatives left at home:	parents
relatives/friends in USA:	none
medical examination:	passed

Your total points out of 40 points:
- More than 34? Very good.
- More than 30? Good.
- Less than 20? Have a look at hthe pages in this chapter again. You CAN do better.

111

Stichwortverzeichnis

A
active voice 8
American English 57, 58, 78
And you really think drugs are fun? 68
Announcement at an American high school 82
articles 29

B
Briefe verfassen 95
British English 57, 58, 78

C
conditional 6
connectives 89
contact clauses 13, 27
Conversations in the school dining room 83

D
defining relative clauses 27
definite articles 29
draft 88
Drugs gain victory over rural areas 61

E
emphasis 65

F
factual texts 60
fictional texts 44
Fragen 22
free text composition 100
future perfect 9

G
gerund 14, 16
Geschichten über Fotos schreiben 100
guided writing 86

H
Hören und verstehen 72

I
improving a text 89
indefinite articles 29
infinitive 16
intelligent guessing 50

L
Lesen und verstehen 44
letters 95

M
mediation 31
Milestones in American History: the Boston Tea Party 74

N
news 72
newspaper articles 106
non-defining relative clauses 27

P
passive voice 8
past perfect 10
prefixes 49
present perfect 24
present perfect progressive 23, 24
pronunciation 78

R
radio 72
Reisebroschüren erstellen 93
relative clauses 26
relative pronouns 13
reported speech 11, 18, 19, 22

S
school systems, German and American 36
spelling 57
Sprachmittlung 31
suffixes 49
summary 64

T
Teenage life in Britain and the USA 79
The last Native American's dream 45

V
Vergangenheit 6, 10, 11, 19

W
Wörterbuch, einsprachiges 105

Z
Zeitungsartikel 106
Zeitverschiebung 11, 18

Besser in

Englisch Lösungsheft
8. Klasse
Gymnasium

 Revision

Wo offene Aufgabenstellungen eine persönliche Antwort erfordern, wurde auf Lösungsvorschläge weitgehend verzichtet.

Exercise 1   Seite 7
1. says – will go
2. don't get – won't let
3. hadn't failed – wouldn't have been
4. shall we go – agree/would we go – agreed (situation may be either real or imaginary)
5. enjoy – will let
6. don't improve – will never allow me to do
7. will have to find – don't pay
8. hadn't bought – I would have saved
9. won – would pay
10. don't let – won't have to think

Exercise 2   Seite 8
1. You can ... if you *get* lost. <u>or</u>: You could ... if you *got* lost.
2. You could ... if you *stayed* ...
3. There wouldn't be ... if he *had lost* ...
4. You can always listen ... if you *go* to ...
5. If you want to get ... you *will* have to take ... (<u>or</u>: ... you *must* take ...)
6. If you *want* ... you can go ...
7. You could visit ... if you *wanted* to.
8. If Prince Charles ever becomes ... the coronation *will* take place ... (<u>or</u>: If he *became* king the coronation *would* take place ...)
9. If you miss ... you *can* still see it later.
10. If the weather *is* fine ... you will really love it.

Exercise 3   Seite 8
1. Our first restaurant will be opened tomorrow. I'm very excited.
2. Did you prepare everything for the opening last week?
3. I bought the water, and the juice was delivered yesterday.
4. Beer is only sold in bottles, but the guests will be given glasses for drinking it.
5. Do you think there will be many guests tomorrow?
6. It will be very full. Twenty people have already booked.
7. Was the big table taken as well?
8. No, the big table is reserved for special guests.
9. Oh, we have to put up the signs that our guests are asked not to smoke.
10. Do you really think we need them? Smoking isn't allowed in any restaurant in this country. Most people know that.
11. Yes, but the law says the signs have to be put up. So let's do it now.

Exercise 4   Seite 9
1. Theo had been followed by the police all day.
2. He had been seen leaving his flat at 7.10 in the morning, taking a bus to Regent Street and entering a travel agency.
3. He came out again at 11 o'clock and was followed by the police to the office where he usually worked.

1 Revision

4. He stayed in the office building until 7 o'clock that evening and then went for a drink with an unknown woman. They drove in her car.
5. At about 11 p.m. he was driven home by her.
6. He was still being followed by the police, but by then they were exhausted.

Exercise 5 Seite 10
1. will already have had
2. will have learned
3. will have written
4. will have been delivered
5. Will you have finished
6. won't have finished it

Exercise 6 Seite 11
1. came back – had already cooked
2. talked – even forgot
3. had worked/had been working – retired
4. phoned – had called
5. phoned – had already left
6. had already met – got home
7. had been playing – had
8. were – liked
9. went upstairs – had already undressed
10. carried – fell

Exercise 7 Seite 12
1. Ben said he <u>was</u> very busy because he <u>had been preparing</u> for the Olympics.
2. Ben claimed that he <u>ran</u> 10 miles every day.
3. He admitted that his last competition in March <u>had been</u> a terrible failure for him.
4. He explained that he <u>was</u> optimistic because he <u>had worked out</u> a new training schedule.
5. Ben explained that before <u>he met/he'd met</u> his new coach he <u>had been training</u> too hard.
6. He promised that he <u>would never make</u> that mistake again.
7. Ben told us that he <u>was/had been</u> so tired one day that he <u>had even fallen/even fell</u> asleep in a restaurant. He added that this <u>had been</u> very embarrassing for him.
8. He said we <u>might not believe him</u>, but <u>he could laugh about it</u> now.

Exercise 8 Seite 13
1. that/which
2. whose
3. which
4. –
5. who
6. –
7. whose
8. which

2 Sprache verstehen

2.1 *The gerund*

Exercise 1 Seite 14
Lösungsvorschlag:
1. There weren't any good seats left, but I didn't mind <u>sitting a little further away from the stage</u>.
2. It was a beautiful play, so I suggested <u>seeing it again</u>.
3. The play was very funny. I couldn't stop <u>laughing</u>.
4. I hope they keep showing it for another few weeks. <u>Changing the programme this late in the summer won't help.</u>

Exercise 2 Seite 15
1. Melissa enjoys working at home.
2. She prefers working in the garden to working in her office.
3. As you know, Melissa loves going to the theatre.
4. But she doesn't mind spending an evening at home either.
5. What she hates most is people who begin doing something and then give it up.
6. She usually avoids talking to people she doesn't like.

Sprache verstehen 2

7. Melissa believes that people who are not nice towards others risk ending up without any friends.
8. That is why she stopped talking badly about other people.
9. Instead she practises being nice to people.
10. For example she recently suggested helping old people in the neighbourhood.

Exercise 3 — Seite 15
1. I like going to the theatre.
2. I also enjoy reading.
3. Watching TV is not my favourite free time activity.
4. Surfing the Internet thoroughly really takes a lot of time.
5. Being nice towards others is important.
6. Because laughing at other people is unkind.
7. I believe that chewing gum in lessons is being rude towards teachers.
8. In my opinion, not saying 'thank you' is one of the rudest things you can do to another person.

2.2 Gerund and/or infinitive?

Exercise 1 — Seite 17
1. Larry: I cannot imagine Michael <u>not coming</u> to school by bike.
2. Peter: Yes, it's hard to believe. But I heard his parents agreed <u>to buy</u> him a new bike.
3. Larry: Really?
4. Peter: Well, the question is easy <u>to answer</u>.
5. Larry: Did you know that Michael even asked me <u>to lend</u> him my bike. He said he hates <u>walking</u>.
6. Peter: Are you thinking about <u>lending</u> him your bike?
7. Larry: I told him that I'm looking forward to <u>seeing</u> him at school, but that I am not willing <u>to lend</u> him my bike at all. It would take me too long <u>to get</u> to school then.

2.3 Reported speech

Exercise 1 — Seite 18
1. The teacher told us to be nice to our families.
2. The teacher told us to remember to say thank you.
3. The teacher told us not to say that we don't like the food.
4. The teacher told us to keep our room clean at all times.
5. The teacher told us to make our beds in the morning.

Exercise 2 — Seite 20
1. Brian told us that he hadn't liked the long train ride the day before.
2. Mr Smith said that everything had been wonderful so far.
3. Tim said that he was a little homesick.
4. Tammy said that she didn't miss anything.
5. Our teacher told us that we would tour London the following day.

Exercise 3 — Seite 21
1. Anne said that she hadn't been to England before.
2. Anne told us that she had spoken a lot of English.
3. Anne told us/said that she'd got a new friend called Rosa.
4. Anne mentioned that she'd had two host sisters in the family.
5. Anne said that she liked/had liked the food a lot.
6. Anne said that she still didn't drink her tea with milk.
7. Anne told us that it had been very sad to say goodbye.
8. Anne reported that she had promised her host sisters that she would send lots of postcards from Germany.
9. Anne told me that in the end she had even cried at the airport.
10. Anne said that she was already planning to go back again the following summer.

Exercise 4 — Seite 22
1. Lucy asked whether she (Anne) would do the trip again.
2. Pete asked (Anne) what the weather had been like.
3. Will asked (Anne) whether there'd been anything that she didn't like/hadn't liked.

3

2 Sprache verstehen

4. Tina asked (Anne) how old her host sisters were/had been.
5. Tom asked (Anne) where she had gone to school.
6. Tina asked Anne whether there had been any nice boys at her school.

2.4 *The present perfect progressive*

Exercise 1 Seite 23
1. have been writing
2. have been learning
3. have been working in Japan
4. have been writing
5. has been travelling
6. has been learning
7. have you been learning
8. have been trying
9. have been sitting
10. have been working

Exercise 2 Seite 25
1. My brother is an actor. He <u>has appeared</u> in a few movies.
2. Is it still raining? – No, <u>it has stopped.</u> (stop)
3. Where have you been? <u>Have you been playing</u> tennis?
4. I <u>have been reading</u> the book you gave me, but I <u>haven't finished</u> it yet.
5. Have you <u>taken</u> the dog for a walk yet?

Exercise 3 Seite 25
Dear Annie,
Thank you so much for your letter. How <u>have you been</u>? I <u>have been</u> really busy lately. I <u>haven't written</u> to you for a while because I <u>have been working</u> hard for school.
Actually, I <u>have</u> just <u>finished</u> preparing for a test tomorrow. Besides my studies, I <u>have</u> also <u>been pursuing</u> my personal interests and hobbies. I <u>have been painting</u> a lot. I think it is important to relax sometimes. I <u>have</u> also <u>been looking</u> around for another, more active hobby, but I <u>haven't found</u> one yet. Do you have any ideas?
Well, I guess it's time for me to get going. I must finish my homework for tomorrow.
I hope to hear from you soon.

Love,
Lisa

2.5 *Relative clauses*

Exercise 1 Seite 26
Hello Listeners,
1. This is a special programme today, dealing with a young girl, Barbara Smith, <u>who</u> has run away from home.
2. Barbara's hair, <u>which</u> she often wears in a ponytail, is brown.
3. Barbara, <u>whose</u> parents are very worried about her disappearance, is 14 years old.
4. Her parents think she ran away because of a bad mark <u>that/which</u> she was given by her English teacher.
5. The police, to <u>whom</u> her parents turned the day after her disappearance, have appealed to the public for help.
6. The bad mark, <u>which</u> she received for not having done her homework once, was not that serious.
7. So Barbara, please know that everything will be OK. Your parents want you to come home, <u>which</u> is what we want, too.

Exercise 2 Seite 28
1. The letter <u>which/that</u> came this morning didn't have a stamp. (defining)
2. Where is the magazine I left on the sofa? (defining)
3. The boy, who had twice been caught stealing money, was seen opening another pupil's school bag. (non-defining). Hier ist eine andere Lösung möglich: The boy seen opening another pupil's school bag had twice been caught stealing money. (defining)
4. Who was the woman you were speaking to? (defining)
5. The car <u>which/that</u> overtook us yesterday didn't have any lights. (defining)
6. My old head teacher, <u>who</u> must be over 70 by now, spoke to me at the match. (non-defining)
7. The ball <u>which/that</u> landed in our garden belonged to our neighbour's children. (defining)

8. This is the dress I bought last summer. (defining)
9. Our neighbour, whose children go to the same school as ours, never speaks to us. (non-defining)
10. The woman who took my bag last week at the hairdresser's knows you. (defining)
11. Did you find the book you were looking for? (defining)
12. The man who came to the door said he was a detective. (defining)
13. The girl who served us in the restaurant was only about 13. (defining)
14. My dad, who retired some years ago, still sometimes teaches at the university. (non-defining)

2.6 Definite/indefinite article

Exercise 1 Seite 30
1. Tina spends a lot of time watching ___ TV.
2. Jodie lay down on the sofa and looked at the picture on the wall.
3. Have you had ___ breakfast yet?
4. Trevor and I arrived at the zoo at the same time.
5. The sun is a star.
6. London is the capital of England.
7. The royal family lives in ___ Buckingham Palace.
8. Where is ___ room 234, please?
9. Our plane leaves from ___ gate 10.
10. She was wearing the hat she bought yesterday.

Exercise 2 Seite 30
1. a – a
2. a – the
3. the – the
4. a
5. an
6. The
7. –
8. a (or –)
9. a

2.7 Mediation

Exercise 1 Seite 31
Lösungsvorschlag:
1. Keine Sorge, das Fläschchen dürfen Sie schon mitnehmen. Nur normale Getränke darf man nicht mitnehmen. Die gibt es – im Gegensatz zu Babymilch – ja im Flugzeug. Aber Ihr Parfüm müssen Sie leider in den Koffer packen, das darf nicht mit an Bord.
2. Ihren Stock dürfen Sie mit ins Flugzeug nehmen. Auch Regenschirme sind erlaubt. Nur Baseball-, Golf- und Hockeyschläger könnten als Waffe missbraucht werden und müssen daher in den Gepäckraum des Flugzeuges.
3. Es tut mir leid, aber das Wasser werden Sie wohl hier trinken müssen. Wie bereits gesagt, ist es nicht erlaubt, Getränkeflaschen mitzunehmen. Und auf Ihre Zahnpasta müssen Sie leider auch verzichten. Aber ich bin mir sicher, dass sie die auch im Flugzeug bekommen können.
4. Sie dürfen alle Ihre Geräte mitnehmen.

Exercise 3 Seite 34
Lösungsvorschlag:
The article says many Chinese families send their children to evening classes after school to improve their chances of reaching university. Politicians have recently criticized these schools and want to call a ban on schools that teach later than 10 p.m.
Not only are the children always tired, because they hardly ever get to sleep before midnight, but the private schools also cost a lot of money, which not every family can afford. Some parents even spend half their income on private tuition. The twenty per cent of children that do not visit evening classes are either too poor or are clever enough not to need extra lessons. But even they will be disadvantaged, because more and more public schools skip parts of the curriculum because they will be taught in the evening classes.

2 Sprache verstehen

Exercise 4   Seite 34

1. Er will wissen, was du gemacht hast, bevor du hierher gekommen bist.
   First he was in New York for three days to do some sightseeing. Afterwards he visited his aunt in Miami for a week. He says he was lucky that she speaks German. Otherwise he would have had a big problem.
2. Sie sagt, dass sie noch nie in Miami war, sich aber vorstellen kann, dass es dort sehr schön sein muss. Sie will wissen, ob du dort am Strand warst.
   Yes, he was at the beach, but only on one day. He had the feeling that mainly old people live there. But he says that might be due to the time of year. No one was on vacation
3. Er möchte wissen, wie dir Kalifornien bisher gefällt. Denkst du, dass es hier anders ist als zuhause in Deutschland?
   Well, he says everything seems to be much bigger here: the streets, the tall houses. He also says it is much noisier downtown and that he has never seen so many people in one place before. He thinks it must be the same in big German cities like Berlin, but since he's a boy from the country he's not used to that.
4. Sie will wissen, was du vorhast dir anzusehen, während du hier bist. Immerhin ist San Francisco eine große Stadt, in der es viele Sehenswürdigkeiten gibt.
   Well, he says he would love to see the Golden Gate Bridge. He has already seen it on TV a couple of times. He believes it might be exciting to finally see it in reality. And he doesn't want to miss out on a ride with a Cable Car. He says the rest of the time he just wants to walk around and take some photos. For him the main thing is that the weather is fine.

Exercise 5   Seite 36

Lösungsvorschlag
für Schlüsselwörter und -begriffe:
German school system: Grundschule (primary education), Hauptschule/Realschule/Gymnasium (different kinds of school for secondary education)

Primary school
- class 1-4 (ages 6-9/10), no more than 30 children
- subjects: reading, writing, maths, science/biology, PE, art, RE (religious education)
- often one teacher for many subjects, class teacher
- elementary English lessons starting from class 2, 3 or 4, singing songs, learning English words for everyday things and topics, speaking first sentences, no grammar or spelling taught
- after primary school each child is given a recommendation for secondary school type (good students: Gymnasium, average students: Realschule, weaker students: Hauptschule)
- recommendations not obligatory, but useful to avoid demotivating experiences

General information
- RE obligatory at German schools (German constitution)
- children are separated into different RE classes, according to their religious denomination (Roman Catholic, Protestant, none/other; ethics: general moral values class)
- no final exams at the end of the school year (except final exams, e.g. for Abitur)
- written exams, tests and marks for involvement in class throughout the whole school year; advantage: student has constant feedback and therefore knows when he or she has to improve in order to pass the year and move up to the next grade
- according to final grades in the report, student can proceed to the next grade (good or average marks) or has to repeat the grade (bad marks)

Gymnasium
- duration: 8-9 years (depending on state)
- Abitur after grade 12 or 13 final examinations
- Hauptschulabschluss (comparable to leaver's certificate, diploma) after 9th grade
- Realschulabschluss (comparable to intermediate high school certificate) after 10th grade
- Fachhochschulreife (entitlement to study at a Fachhochschule/university of applied science) after 12th grade

- two foreign languages obligatory (mostly English, French, Latin, classical Greek, Spanish, Italian, depending on school)

Hauptschule/Realschule
- final examinations after grade 9/10 (without a pass, no diploma)
- only one foreign language obligatory
- change from Hauptschule to Realschule or Realschule to Gymnasium (and vice versa) possible, depending on student's grades
- less complex and demanding way of learning (compared to Gymnasium) more time to learn, more help given by teachers, lower standard
- A and B classes for main subjects; according to qualifications of students separation into upper and lower level classes in each main subject, better support in line with the student's requirements

Gesamtschule (comprehensive school, comparable to high school)
- combination of all three German school types
- main subjects are taught in classes structured according to the level of each of the three separate school types, students being sorted into these three levels according to their abilities in the subject (sorting takes place each half year)
- advantage: easy to change between the three school types without having to change schools.

Exercise 6   Seite 38
Lösungsvorschlag:
The German school system is divided into two levels: primary and secondary. There are three different kinds of schools to which students in secondary education can go, according to their abilities: Hauptschule, Realschule or Gymnasium. All German children start their education in primary school when they are about six years old. The main subjects – apart from learning how to read and write – are Maths, Science/Biology, PE, Art and RE (religious education) and elementary English.
After primary school each child is given a recommendation for one of the three types of secondary school. Good students are usually sent to a Gymnasium, average students to a Realschule and weaker students are given the recommendation for Hauptschule. Although these recommendations are not obligatory they are useful in order to avoid demotivating experiences.
Unlike in other countries, the UK for example, there are no final exams at the end of the term or school year in Germany, other than the school leaving exams for the Hauptschule, or Realschule and the Abitur (the final examination at the Gymnasium which qualifies for university). German children have to write exams and tests regularly throughout the school year. The advantage is that each student has a constant feedback. Depending on the final grades in their annual reports, students can proceed to the next grade (good or average marks) or have to repeat the grade (bad marks).
The Gymnasium usually has a duration of 8-9 years, depending on the state. If a student does not want to sit the Abitur or feels that he or she might not be able to pass it, it is possible to leave the Gymnasium one year before the Abitur with a certificate that enables a student to study at a university of applied science.
For students at the Gymnasium two foreign languages are obligatory. Depending on the offers available, most German students decide to start with English, French or Latin as their first foreign language.
Students at a Hauptschule or Realschule only have to learn one foreign language, but they may choose to learn a second one if they want. Learning a second foreign language also offers them the chance to change to a Gymnasium if their marks are good enough.
A combination of all three German school types is the Gesamtschule, which can be compared to a high school or a comprehensive school (UK). The main subjects are taught in classes which correspond to the level of each of the three traditional school types. Each term (or half year) students are sorted into these three levels according to their abilities in the various subjects. A big advantage of this kind of combined school is that it is easy for students to change between the three school types, e.g. if a student decides to take the

2 Sprache verstehen

Abitur, since he/she does not then have to change school and settle in.

Exercise 8   Seite 39
Lösungsvorschlag:
Das amerikanische Schulsystem unterscheidet sich von dem vieler anderer Länder. Erziehung und Bildung sind in erster Linie Aufgabe des Staates und der örtlichen Regierungen: Die einzelnen Staaten haben die Kontrolle darüber, was in ihren Schulen unterrichtet wird sowie über die Anforderungen, denen ein Schüler entsprechen muss. Außerdem sind die einzelnen Staaten verantwortlich für die Finanzierung ihrer Schulen. Dennoch gibt es einige Faktoren, in denen alle amerikanischen Schulen übereinstimmen, wie z. B. die Einteilung des Bildungssystems in drei Stufen: primäre Bildung (Grundschulen), sekundäre Bildung (weiterführende Schulen) und höhere Bildung (Fachoberschulen und Universitäten).
Normalerweise geht ein amerikanischer Schüler zwölf Jahre lang zur Schule. Die Schulpflicht hingegen endet in den meisten Bundesstaaten im Alter von 16 Jahren. Alle Kinder in den Vereinigten Staaten von Amerika haben Zugang zu gebührenfreien staatlichen Schulen. Privatschulen (kirchliche und konfessionsunabhängige) gibt es zwar, jedoch müssen Schüler an diesen Schulen Schulgelder bezahlen.
Die meisten amerikanischen Kinder beginnen ihre Schulbildung noch bevor sie eine Regelschule besuchen, und zwar in einer (privaten) Vorschule oder im Kindergarten.
Im Alter von etwa sechs Jahren besuchen amerikanische Kinder dann die Grundschule.
Nach der Grundschule gehen die meisten Kinder in die sogenannte Mittelschule. Ihre Fächer können sich die Schüler weitgehend selbst aussuchen.
Anschließend gehen die Schüler vier Jahre lang auf die High School, bis sie im Alter von etwa 17 Jahren bzw. nach der 12. Klasse den Abschluss, ihr High School Diplom bekommen. Eine Besonderheit amerikanischer Schulen ist, dass es für jede Klassenstufe an der High School eigene Namen gibt. So heißt ein Schüler im ersten Jahr an der High School *freshman*, im zweiten Jahr *sophomore*, im dritten Jahr *junior* und im vierten und letzten Jahr *senior*.
Je höher die Klassenstufe, desto mehr Fächer gibt es, aus denen man wählen kann. Für jeden erfolgreich abgeschlossenen Kurs gibt es Punkte (*credits*). Um den Schulabschluss zu schaffen und ihr Abschlussdiplom überreicht zu bekommen, müssen sich die Schüler eine gewisse Anzahl dieser Leistungspunkte verdienen. Eine Abschlussprüfung wie in vielen anderen Ländern (z. B. Deutschland), gibt es nicht. Die Anzahl der zu wählenden Kurse und die Kombinationsmöglichkeiten variieren, je nach Schulbezirk und angestrebtem Diplom.
Nur mit einem High-School-Diplom kann man sich an einer der Universitäten des Landes einschreiben. Außerdem ist es wichtig zu wissen, dass Fachoberschulen (*colleges*) und Universitäten (*universities*) manchmal ganz bestimmte *high school credits* (Leistungspunkte) verlangen oder auch Aufnahmeprüfungen durchführen, bevor sie Studenten zulassen. Das bedeutet, dass amerikanische Schüler schon früh ihre Karrierepläne im Kopf haben müssen, um diese speziellen Anforderungen erfüllen zu können. Aus diesem Grund hat jede High School mindestens einen *guidance counselor*. Das ist ein Karriereberater, meist ein Lehrer, der den Schülern mit ihren Karriereplänen weiterhilft und sie berät.

Test

Exercise 1   Seite 40
1. lending
2. to phone
3. to give
4. leaving
5. saying
6. working
7. to become
8. reading

Texte verstehen 3

Exercise 2   Seite 40
1. He drank water which/that contained bacteria.
2. His car, whose engine had been checked the week before, broke down.
3. Maria, who(m) he is soon going to marry, suddenly felt sick when they wanted to go to the cinema.
4. The television (which) he wanted to buy was already sold.
5. Maria's dog bit his hand/bit him in the hand, which was nothing new to him.

Exercise 3   Seite 41
1. –/a/a/the
2. the/a/the/–
3. a/a/–/–
4. the/an/–/the/the/the/the

Exercise 4   Seite 41
1. haven't seen
2. look/are looking
3. Do you want – are you
4. am going
5. do you go
6. do you go?
7. have (got) – cuts
8. is still – have started to work/working
9. is – spoke – were thinking – attending – Did you go?

10. worked/used to work – lost – didn't have
11. Has he managed
12. didn't take – am still keen – could go – wanted
13. do – Have you heard/Did you hear – died
14. am – wasn't/was not
15. mustn't/must not

Exercise 5   Seite 42
1. has always wanted
2. has never been
3. has been looking forward
4. has agreed
5. has come
6. has been waiting
7. has been sitting
8. has been talking – have been drinking
9. have you been – have been trying
10. have just had
11. have been standing
12. has had

Exercise 6   Seite 43
1. ... he had been sitting in the pub with Robert when Emma phoned.
2. ... had asked him where he had been all the time.
3. ... could tell she was very angry about having to wait out in the cold.

3   Texte verstehen

3.1 Lesen und verstehen

The last Native American's dream

Exercise 2   Seite 47

Who?	The mixed-blood Jimmy; Chief Sitting Bull; Chief Spotted Elk, known as Big Foot; the Sioux; Colonel James W. Forsyth; Black Coyote; U.S. troops/soldiers; Jimmy's mother
What?	The Ghost Dance of the Sioux; Native Americans ("Indians") fighting against the U.S. American troops; Chief Sitting Bull's arrest; the relocation of the Sioux to a military base in Omaha; the search for weapons amongst the Sioux by the U.S. soldiers; Black Coyote's refusal to hand over his Winchester gun; the Wounded Knee Massacre
When?	December 1890; (massacre on December 29, 1890)
Where?	Standing Rock Reservation in South Dakota; Wounded Knee, a place close to a river at the Pine Ridge Reservation in South Dakota
Why?	The U.S. Americans, who put the Native Americans into reservations, were afraid of the Ghost Dance. The Native Americans simply wanted to be free.

3 Texte verstehen

Exercise 3 Seite 47
Lösungsvorschlag:
1. lines 1–3 Jimmy's foresight – something bad is going to happen (Introduction)
2. lines 4–13 Facts about Jimmy – half Native American, half white
3. lines 14–21 The Ghost Dance
4. lines 22–36 Sitting Bull's arrest and his dream
5. lines 37–41 Jimmy's attempt to help his people
6. lines 42–50 Colonel James W. Forsyth takes control over the Native Americans
7. lines 51–55 Black Coyote's fatal mistake (Climax)
8. lines 56–60 Wounded Knee Massacre
9. lines 61–68 The life of the buffalo hunters is over (Ending)

Exercise 4 Seite 48
Lösungsvorschlag:
1. The U.S. troops arrest Chief Sitting Bull because the American settlers are afraid of <u>the Sioux dancing the Ghost Dance</u>. They do not want to hurt him; their plan is just to <u>arrest Sitting Bull until the Sioux calm down and stop scaring the white people with the Ghost Dance</u>.
2. They dance the Ghost Dance to <u>call on their dead ancestors for help, because they know that there will be a fight against the white men and they need more power. Probably they have fewer men than the U.S. soldiers.</u>
3. He dreams that he will die at the hands of his own people. (That is why the Native Americans in the reservation make Jimmy responsible for Sitting Bull's death. Of course, it is not Jimmy's fault; he just translates for the U.S. soldiers.)
4. The soldiers find a Winchester gun. Black Coyote does not want to give it to the soldiers because he had to pay a lot for it. When the soldiers try to take it away from him, a shot goes off. The soldiers think Black Coyote is shooting at them, so they fire back.
5. The sad result of this day's happenings is that about 300 Sioux and <u>twenty-five soldiers died</u>. <u>(Ever since people talk of the Wounded Knee Massacre.)</u>
6. Sitting Bull's last words are "<u>I am the last Indian</u>" and he is right in the end because the Native Americans are put into <u>reservations. They have to live there and the white people influence their lives. Many Native Americans die in the so-called 'Indian wars' with the white men.</u>

Exercise 5 Seite 49

translator		Übersetzer
reservation		Reservat
terrified		erschrocken, verängstigt, entsetzt
warriors		Krieger
troops		Truppen
hatred	hate	Hass
(to) arrest		verhaften
loss		Verlust
(to) foresee		vorhersehen
grave		ernst, schwerwiegend
sadness	sad	Traurigkeit
relocate		relokalisieren, umsiedeln, verlegen
massacre		Massaker, Blutbad, Gemetzel

Exercise 6 Seite 49

skin	Haut
(to) spread	ausbreiten, sich verbreiten
Chief	Häuptling
tribe	Stamm
traitor	Verräter
ancestors	Vorfahren, Stammväter
(to) creep	kriechen
rifles	Waffen, Gewehre
(to) refuse	ablehnen, sich weigern
on purpose	absichtlich
threatened	bedroht, gefährdet

Exercise 7 Seite 50
Lösungsvorschlag:
Die Geschichte „The last Native American's dream" – Der Traum des letzten Indianers – handelt von dem jungen Mann Jimmy, der halb Indianer, halb Weißer ist. Jimmy wusste nie, in welche Welt er gehört. Als Jimmy alt genug war, verließ er das Reservat, um für die Amerikaner als Übersetzer zu arbeiten. Aber die sehen nur den Indianer in ihm. Jimmy ist einsam.

Texte verstehen 3

Eines Tages verbreitet die Nachricht, dass die Indianer den Geistertanz tanzen, Angst und Schrecken unter den amerikanischen Soldaten. Jimmy versucht, ihnen zu erklären, dass es sich beim Geistertanz nur um eine Art Gebet handelt, bei dem die Toten zu Hilfe gerufen werden sollen. Aber die Amerikaner beschließen, Häuptling Sitting Bull (Sitzender Bulle) vom Standing Rock Reservat zu verhaften, bis sich die Lage beruhigt hat. Doch etwas geht schief. Beim Versuch, ihn zu verhaften, wird Sitting Bull getötet. Jimmys Stamm hält ihn für einen Verräter, da Jimmy als Übersetzer dabei war. Sitting Bull hatte kurz vor seinem Tod einen Traum, in dem er gesehen hatte, dass er durch jemandem von seinem eigenen Volk sterben würde. Seine letzten Worte waren „Ich bin der letzte Indianer." Jimmy beschließt, dass er seinem Volk helfen wird, indem er für die Indianer bei den Amerikanern vorspricht.

Doch Jimmys Bemühungen helfen nicht. Am 29. Dezember 1890 gibt Oberst James W. Forsyth den Befehl, die Sioux in ein Militärlager in Omaha umzusiedeln, um sie unter Kontrolle zu haben. Unterwegs rasten sie bei Wounded Knee (Verwundetes Knie), einem Platz in der Nähe eines Flusses im Pine Ridge Reservat in South Dakota.

Um sicherzugehen, dass niemand verletzt wird, verlangt der Oberst von den Indianern die Übergabe ihrer Waffen. Der Krieger Black Coyote (Schwarzer Steppenwolf) weigert sich, sein Gewehr herauszugeben. Dabei löst sich versehentlich ein Schuss. Die Truppen glauben, sie werden angegriffen, und feuern zurück. Es folgt ein Massaker: Etwa 300 Sioux-Indianer, unter ihnen Häuptling Big Foot, und 25 Soldaten verloren ihr Leben.

Jimmy denkt einige Zeit nach dem Massaker am Ufer des Flusses Wounded Knee Creek über die letzten Worte von Sitting Bull nach: „Ich bin der letzte Indianer." Er erkennt, dass der alte Häuptling recht behalten hat. Der Tod von Sitting Bull kennzeichnete das Ende eines Zeitalters, das Massaker von Wounded Knee aber steht für das Ende einer Kultur.

The Tanaeka ritual

Exercise 2 Seite 53

Lösungsvorschläge:
1. lines 1–6   Facts about John – Native American, belongs to the Kaw Nation
2. lines 7–17   More space for the Kaw Nation is needed
3. lines 18–32   The tradition of Tanaeka – an endurance ritual
4. lines 33–44   The rules of Tanaeka
5. lines 45–50   John's lessons
6. lines 51–63   Survival techniques
7. lines 64–74   The secret of the Tanaeka of the 21st century
8. lines 75–85   Peter's help
9. lines 86–92   Six days in the cave
10. lines 92–95   Homecoming
11. lines 95–102 The pocket money

Exercise 3 Seite 53

1. John, a thirteen year-old Native American; his grandfather; his brother Peter; his sister Emma; his mother
2. John's grandfather wants him to undergo the ritual of Tanaeka, a traditional ceremony which turns a boy into a man. John has to be in the wilds alone for six days. He has to live on what nature provides, and therefore has to learn everything he needs to know from his grandfather. But in the end he gets some help from his brother.
3. Modern times, twenty-first century
4. Kaw City, in a reservation for Native Americans of "The Kaw Nation", northern Oklahoma, U.S.A.
5. John has to take Tanaeka because his grandfather believes in the old traditions. Even if it is not necessary in modern times to undergo that ritual, and John and the younger members of his family do not understand why he has to do it. That is why John and Peter decide to cheat (= mogeln). This way the grandfather can stick to his traditions and the boys do not have to suffer.

3 Texte verstehen

Exercise 4   Seite 54
1. gewöhnlich, normal, üblich
2. staatlich anerkannt, von der Regierung anerkannt
3. erschaffen, schaffen
4. ertränken; ertrinken
5. Biber
6. Wasserschildkröte
7. vergrößern
8. an etwas teilnehmen, bei etwas mitmachen
9. beweisen
10. jagen
11. (wilde) Kräuter
12. versorgen, ausstatten mit, zur Verfügung stellen
13. sich ernähren von, leben von
14. Beere
15. Heuschrecke, Grashüpfer
16. Käfer
17. nahrhaft
18. essbar
19. giftige Schlange
20. nackt
21. roh
22. Aufmerksamkeit schenken, aufpassen
23. eklig, Ekel erregend
24. Albtraum
25. tarnen, verkleiden, maskieren
26. bestehen auf, verlangen
27. mampfen
28. eifrig
29. (jemanden/jemandes Stimme) nachmachen, nachahmen, imitieren
30. elend, jämmerlich, erbärmlich, kläglich, traurig
31. Dosenessen, Konserven
32. am Leben halten, unterstützen
33. Dessert, Nachtisch
34. stolz auf
35. schlechtes Gewissen
36. mit jemandem quitt sein

Exercise 5   Seite 55
1. The 'nowadays' indicates that in former times … the tribe was not seen as an independent nation by the Americans. They were treated like second-class people, which still can be seen in the fact that they live in a reservation.
2. The fact that the grandfather never spoke Sioux among people who did not understand it shows that he … was a very polite person since he did not talk in a language that the people around did not understand.
3. His "worst nightmare" is … having to live on grasshoppers and beetles for some days as well as having to look after himself (making fire, finding a place to sleep etc). That shows us that he is a modern person who likes the comfort of city life.
4. It is very unlikely that he will meet a white person in the reservation because … normally white men do not come into the reservation. There is no trade and no war with the white people anymore.
5. Peter's real intention was to … speak to John alone because he wanted to give him advice for his time in the wilderness.
6. The secret of the Tanaeka of the twenty-first century is … to cheat. You can hide proper food somewhere so that you can survive without having to hunt or eat beetles. It's a combination of tradition and modern lifestyle. (But of course then it does not have anything to do with the original ritual anymore).
7. If you cannot believe your eyes … you see something which you think cannot be true, because it is either too good or too bad. You think it must be a dream.
8. John wants to express with this sentence that … he was very happy that his brother had prepared the surprise for him in the cave. He had not expected anything like that and thanked his brother for it in his thoughts. Of course, he had always loved his brother.
9. If Peter … had eaten too much he would have looked very healthy and not as if he had lived on beetles, berries and wild animals. To hunt an animal you usually have to run a lot, which means that you lose weight. So his grandfather would have known that he had cheated.
10. Peter feels guilty because … his grandfather is so happy that he passed his Tanaeka. He could feel very proud himself, if he hadn't cheated. So he knows that he does not deserve his family's approval (= Lob).

Texte verstehen 3

Exercise 6 Seite 57
1. Right
2. Wrong: The ceremony turns a boy into a man.
3. Wrong: According to the legend the island on which the Kaw people lived was too small, so fathers had to drown their children and the women prayed for help.
4. Wrong: Legend says that beavers and turtles enlarged the island.
5. Right
6. Wrong: Peter only tells John that he survived his Tanaeka, too. (Later John finds out that it was not hard at all, because Peter cheated.)
7. Right
8. Wrong: He pays attention to everything his grandfather tells him.
9. Wrong: John's mother feels pity with him and tries to persuade his grandfather that John should not have to do it. But she doesn't resist when he insists on John having to undergo the ritual.
10. Right
11. Wrong: After six days John goes back to his family.
12. Wrong: Peter buys all the food for John and later tells him that they are quits now because John lent him the money he needed to buy the food and equipment for his own Tanaeka and Peter never paid the money back to John.

Exercise 7 Seite 58
1. to criticise
2. neighbour
3. catalogue
4. centre
5. travelling
6. flavour
7. Mum
8. harbour
9. theatre
10. dialogue
11. colour
12. programme

Exercise 8 Seite 59
1. Ht
2. Ze
3. Ox
4. Sh
5. Bq
6. Wm
7. Ay
8. Qb
9. Kz
10. Ud
11. Dp
12. Cj
13. Ya
14. Ev
15. Gs
16. Tw
17. Jn
18. Mu
19. Xf
20. Fr
21. Ic
22. Ll
23. Pg
24. Nk
25. Vi
26. Ro

Drugs gain victory over rural areas

Exercise 1 Seite 61
Paragraph 1, lines 1–8: little village of Bloxham in Oxfordshire ... fifteen year old Lindsay Bradford ... found ... with an overdose of cocaine

Paragraph 2, lines 9–15: parents ... association against drug-abuse among teenagers

Paragraph 3, lines 16–24: frustrated and bored young people ... British Crime Survey ... at least 6 % of youngsters in the countryside take class A drugs

Paragraph 4, lines 25–38: peer group pressure ... boredom of life in a small village

Paragraph 5, lines 39–48: Drug-taking ... routine part of village life for teenagers ...'Bloxham Initiative against Drug-Abuse' (BlaDA)

Paragraph 6, lines 49–58: build a new youth centre ... offer activities ... offer help ...Observe ... be aware ... take the initiative

Exercise 2 Seite 62
1. no
2. yes
3. yes
4. no
5. no
6. yes
7. yes
8. no

Exercise 3 Seite 63
1. T
2. I (großes i)
3. d
4. P
5. m
6. e
7. X
8. A
9. o
10. Y
11. V
12. a
13. B
14. j
15. b
16. g
17. L
18. D
19. l (kleines L)
20. J
21. k
22. c
23. C
24. F
25. K
26. h
27. n
28. W
29. E
30. H
31. f
32. N
33. R
34. G
35. Q
36. S
37. M
38. Z
39. O
40. i
41. U

13

3 Texte verstehen

Exercise 4   Seite 64

Paragraph 1	Village girl on drugs
Paragraph 2	Shocked parents form association against drug abuse
Paragraph 3	Drug problems in the countryside almost as high as in cities
Paragraph 4	Boredom and peer group pressure changed Lindsay's life
Paragraph 5	Drugs – a routine part of village life
Paragraph 6	Bloxham Initiative's plans to keep teenagers off drugs

Exercise 5   Seite 65
Lösungsvorschlag:
The newspaper article "Drugs gain victory over rural areas" deals with the problem of drug abuse by teenagers in rural areas. For the inhabitants of the Oxfordshire village of Bloxham the countryside no longer seems to stand for a safe and happy childhood after fifteen year old Lindsay Bradford is/was found with an overdose of cocaine in a school playground.
Shocked by the tragedy, parents and villagers start/have started an association against teenage drug abuse (BlaDA = Bloxham Initiative against Drug Abuse).
The article states that living in the countryside no longer protects teenagers against urban drug problems. Levels of drug consumption are almost as high as in inner city areas.
And it is not only the poor or uneducated that turn to drugs. Lindsay's parents claim that they noticed a change in her behaviour but felt helpless, especially after she had run away from home. They see the reasons for her problems in peer group pressure and boredom.
Professor Mark Rellis, director of the Centre for Public Health at Oxford University, claims that it is also very easy for today's teenagers to get information on, and access to, drugs.
Rural teenagers themselves report that they take to drugs because there is little else for them to do in their villages. To combat this, BlaDA spokesperson Larry White says the association plans to offer teenagers more sensible free-time activities with the help of volunteers and a new youth centre. Observance, awareness and involvement – the basis of BlaDA's strategy – will also include help for affected families.

Exercise 6   Seite 65

1. Nichts, worüber man sich Sorgen machen musste, keine Autos, keine Fremden, solange ich nur rechtzeitig zuhause war, war alles in Ordnung.
2. Es ist nun drei Wochen her, dass die 15-jährige Lindsay Bradford mit einer Überdosis Kokain auf dem Spielplatz der örtlichen Grundschule gefunden wurde.
3. Das Mädchen wurde in letzter Minute ins Krankenhaus gebracht und erholt sich nun in einer Klinik, die auf junge Menschen mit Drogenproblemen spezialisiert ist.
4. Jeder muss sich engagieren, wenn wir wirklich etwas verändern wollen.
5. Die idyllischen Häuschen und malerischen Dörfer auf dem Land verdecken/verstecken/verbergen oft eine Vielzahl von tiefer liegenden Problemen, besonders die der frustrierten und gelangweilten jungen Menschen, die sich in ständig wachsender Zahl Drogen und Kriminalität zuwenden.
6. Sie begann Lügen zu erzählen, wohin sie ging und mit wem sie zusammen war – schwer zu überprüfen, da wir nur über ihr Handy mit ihr Kontakt aufnehmen konnten.
7. Die Familie führt Lindsays Probleme auf Gruppenzwang und die Langeweile des Lebens in einem kleinen Dorf zurück.
8. Wir wollen sowohl den Kindern als auch den Eltern zeigen, dass sie nicht allein sind und dass wir es zusammen schaffen können.

Texte verstehen 3

Exercise 7 — Seite 66
1. We do need a better programme for our teenagers to keep them off drugs.
2. Do let me know if you want me to offer an activity.
3. We did notice but there was nothing we could do.
4. Lindsay: I did want to stop taking drugs but I just couldn't.
5. Cathy: I did want to call you earlier but you had been so strange when we last saw each other.
6. I really do believe that we can change something in our community.
7. I did hear what my parents told me about drugs but I didn't want to listen.
8. I never believed how dangerous drugs can be, but I do know better now.

Exercise 8 — Seite 67
1. No, thank you Mum. I can call her myself.
2. Why don't you try (to do) it yourself?
3. Yes, Lindsay repaired it herself.
4. He cut it himself.
5. You have to look after yourselves.
6. Your mother and I are old enough to look after ourselves.
7. No, they asked us themselves.
8. No, it wasn't. She had the idea herself.
9. Yes, we did. And I told her that I could never do it myself. I'd be too embarrassed.

Test

Exercise 1 — Seite 68
1. c. 2. b. 3. c. 4. a. 5. c.

Exercise 2 — Seite 69
1. This belongs to the process of growing up. (ll. 11–12)
2. ... if I did (it). (l. 27)
3. He seemed not to care about anything. (l. 18–19)
4. One won't make you addicted! (l. 3)
5. I knew there was something going on. (ll. 24–25)
6. She was suffering from withdrawal symptoms. (l. 30)
7. Cool, I've always wanted to try that! (l. 5)
8. ... apart from in lessons. (l. 23)

Exercise 3 — Seite 70
Lösungsvorschlag:
1. ... they are afraid of what their friends might think of them: they are not daring, they are boring and want to spoil their fun.
2. ... she has been in the situation herself: some people who she thought were her friends offered her drugs.
3. ... they would only make a junkie out of people who are not as strong and well-informed as herself.
4. ... her best friend Lindsay took an overdose of cocaine.
5. ... Lindsay stopped doing her homework and was not interested in spending time with her old friends anymore.
6. ... Lindsay has recovered and finally learned that drugs are dangerous – not fun.
7. ... pity because they are unable to see that drugs ruin their lives.
8. ... be happy to be healthy, have friends and the chance to lead a good life.

Exercise 4 — Seite 70

No	German	BE	AE
1.	Hosen	trousers	pants
2.	Gefängnis	prison	jail
3.	im Stadtzentrum	in the city centre	downtown
4.	üben	(to) practise	(to) practice
5.	Straßenkreuzung	crossroads	intersection
6.	Müll	rubbish	trash, garbage
7.	Nachbarschaft	neighbourhood	neighborhood
8.	Pommes	chips	(French) fries
9.	Wohnwagen	caravan	trailer
10.	Geschmacksrichtung	flavour	flavor
11.	Kino	cinema	movies/ movie theater

15

3 Texte verstehen

12. Taxi	taxi	cab
13. Schlafanzug	pyjamas	pajamas
14. Handy	mobile (phone)	cell phone
15. Geschäft, Laden	shop	store
16. Ferien/Urlaub	holiday(s)	vacation
17. Süßigkeiten	sweets	candy
18. Benzin	petrol	gas
19. Fußball	football	soccer
20. Geldschein	note	bill

Exercise 5 Seite 71

Dear Lindsay,

I hope you are feeling better. Don't worry; we have not forgotten you. Yesterday all the pupils in our year went to the city centre to go to the theatre. Only Lucy had to stay at home because she was ill. We had to wait in a long queue before we were allowed to go in. Mrs Peters said it would be an interesting programme, but we thought it was rubbish. We ate lots of sweets and biscuits; you know that I especially like the ones with chocolate flavour. After the play we wanted to go to the harbour, but the underground was closed for repair works, so we had to take taxis. There were not enough seats, so Nigel decided to sit in the boot. Can you imagine the colour of Mrs Peters' face when she saw him climbing into it? "We have to have a dialogue in private young man!" she said. Then she even called his mum on her mobile phone. Poor Nigel! By the way, we are planning a big party for you as soon as you get home again. So get well soon!

Lots of love, Cathy

3.2 Hören und verstehen
Milestones in American History: the Boston Tea Party

Exercise 1 Seite 74

Lösungsvorschlag:
Title: ... milestones in American history. Milestones are important events.
Introduction: ... radio report, in which an expert will give information about a famous incident in American history.
He will talk about the Boston Tea Party. He will tell me what happened and how and why, and give me some background information on the British colonies in 18th century New England.
I know something about British colonies in New England: that the first colonies were founded close to the East coast. Many settlers came to New England to gain religious freedom. Life was hard in the New World because of the different conditions (weather, food, lifestyle, ...), but soon towns were established and life improved. The more people came, the less space they had, so the colonists started to go westward. Land was taken away from the Native Americans and the British government had to send soldiers to protect the settlers.

Exercise 2 Seite 75
1. true
2. false: book about the Boston Tea Party
3. true
4. not in text.
5. true
6. false: British East India Company
7. false: Because smugglers were importing tea from Holland the company didn't have any prospect of selling its tea in England.
8. true
9. not in text
10. true
11. false: They were only disguised as Native Americans on December 16, 1773
12. not in text

Texte verstehen 3

Exercise 3 — Seite 76
1. The name of the radio programme is "What America Wants to Know".
2. The British Crown faced debts of £132 million.
3. In 1764 both the Sugar Act and the Stamp Act were introduced.
4. There was so much tea rotting in London warehouses in 1773 because the colonists had boycotted tea sold by the East India Company.
5. c.
6. c.
7. b.
8. c.
9. a.
10. b.

Exercise 4 — Seite 77
1. E   4. A   7. G   10. D
2. C   5. F   8. I
3. H   6. J   9. B

Exercise 6 — Seite 78
1. AE   3. AE   5. BE   7. AE
2. BE   4. AE   6. BE   8. both

Teenage life in Britain and the USA

Exercise 1 — Seite 79
1. AE   3. BE   5. BE
2. BE   4. AE   6. BE

Exercise 2 — Seite 79

Name	school	family	hobbies
Stacy		✔	✔
Nolan	✔		✔
Paula		✔	✔
Dean			✔
Susan	✔	✔	✔
D.J.	✘	✔	✔

Name	friends	daily routine	facts about his/her region
Stacy	(✔)	✔	✔
Nolan	✔	✔	
Paula	✔	✔	
Dean			✔
Susan	✔	(✔)	
D.J.	(✔)		

Stop: Mistake!

Exercise 1 — Seite 80
1. Mariella says that her class found many differences between the schools in the three countries, but that teenagers' lives in general are more or less the same everywhere.
2. She explains that in Germany you can take your Abitur after twelve or thirteen years at school, depending on the state you live in.
3. Mariella's class has lessons in the afternoon only once a week, on Wednesdays.
4. The lunch break at their school is between 1 p.m. and 1.45 p.m. and because they don't have a school cafeteria every pupil has to bring his or her own lunch.
5. Mariella says German pupils often learn to play an instrument at their local music school.
6. She says that like British or American teenagers, German teenagers like to spend their free time with their friends.

Exercise 2 — Seite 81
1. don't hesitate to …
2. since it allows you to …
3. I am talking for …
4. comparable to …
5. mostly
6. there are many differences
7. depending on …
8. up to four times a week
9. strangely
10. luckily

Exercise 3 — Seite 81
1. Es war sehr interessant für uns, etwas über euer Leben zu hören/erfahren.
2. Vor allem, was das Schulleben betrifft.
3. Seltsamerweise scheinen Teenager/junge Menschen außerhalb der Schule überall auf der Welt gleich zu sein.
4. Wenn man sein Abitur machen möchte – welches vergleichbar mit den A-Levels in Großbritannien oder dem High-School-Abschluss in Amerika ist, da es einen dazu befähigt, zur Universität zu gehen –, muss man aufs Gymnasium gehen.

17

3 Texte verstehen

5. An diesen Schulen werden die Schüler in den meisten Fächern in verschiedene Gruppen (ein)geteilt, je nach ihren Fähigkeiten.
6. Wir haben einen unterschiedlichen Stundenplan für jeden Tag der Woche, aber dieser wiederholt sich jede Woche, das ganze Schuljahr lang.
7. Da wir keine Mensa haben, muss jeder Schüler/jede Schülerin das eigene Mittagessen mitbringen.
8. Oh, und falls ihr jetzt neidisch seid, dass die Schule in Deutschland so früh aufhört/zu Ende ist: Wir fangen auch früh an!
9. Wenn man an keiner dieser AGs Interesse hat, kann man nach seinem Unterricht/seiner letzten Schulstunde nach Hause gehen.
10. Zögert nicht, uns weitere Fragen zu stellen!

Test

Exercise 1 Seite 82

	Topic	Yes	No
1.	Birthday congratulations	✔	
2.	Principal's complaints about students' behavior		✔
3.	Mother looking for child		✔
4.	Party preparations of older students	✔	
5.	Opening times of 'lost and found' office		✔
6.	Results of school team in knowledge competition	✔	
7.	Extra meeting times for clubs because of a special event	✔	
8.	Search for students that should be in class		✔

Exercise 2 Seite 82
1. B   3. C   5. A   7. A
2. C   4. B   6. A   8. C

Exercise 3 Seite 83
1. F   5. E   9. M   13. I
2. N   6. L   10. D 14. G
3. B   7. A   11. K
4. J   8. H   12. C

Exercise 4 Seite 84
1. Wrong: A boy says that no one could have expected the game to be such a disaster. He says he knew that the team would have problems beating Bristol School.
2. Correct
3. Wrong: The second boy tells the other not to be unfair, because Jim did not hurt himself on purpose. It was an accident.
4. Wrong: The first boy thinks that.
5. Wrong: The first boy says that they can be glad that the season is nearly over and he hopes that Jim will be well again after the summer.
6. Correct
7. Correct
8. Wrong: Brian tells the girls that his team really wanted to win. The situation was exciting because there was no topic left that he and his team members were good at.
9. Wrong: Brian says Sarah is the specialist on politics and Luke is good at sports questions.
10. Wrong: Brian describes how he did not even listen to the end of the question because he knew the answer to that question from an exam in his biology class, so he could answer it even before the question was read out completely.

Texte schreiben 4

4.1 Mit vorgegebenen Informationen Texte erstellen

Exercise 2   Seite 87

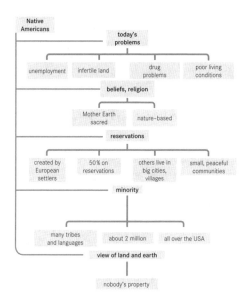

Exercise 3   Seite 89

Lösungsvorschlag für einen ausgearbeiteten Text:
It all started when European settlers took over the fertile land and put the Native Americans into reservations. Even though some two million Native Americans live in the USA, they are a minority. And they are split into different tribes, each tribe speaking its own language.

Their religion is nature-based. The Native Americans believe that every kind of animal or plant is holy and has to be treated as such, because it all belongs to the universe of the Great Spirit (comparable to the Christian God). If one part of this cosmos is disturbed, the whole cosmos is affected. Native Americans can read the signs of nature, so they closely observe, for example, the behavior of animals or the growth of plants.

Plants, animals, humans, everything comes from and lives off the earth. That is why Mother Earth is sacred in their belief; and with it everything that comes from it.

Nowadays about 50% of all Native Americans still live in the generally small and peaceful communities in the reservations. The rest live in villages or in big cities outside the reservations.

They have to face a lot of problems, some of which date back to the time when the "white man" first appeared on their land. As mentioned above, the European settlers took away the fertile land from the Natives. The reservations were usually established on soil which was infertile and therefore useless for the Europeans. Neither the location of the reservations nor the soil has changed ever since, so Native Americans still suffer from the infertile land they live on.

They can hardly cultivate any food so they have to buy everything.

Another big problem is that ever since "white men" introduced Native Americans to alcohol – trading it for leather and furs – many have been addicted to alcohol and other drugs.

Alcoholism is also the result of another major problem: unemployment. Many Native Americans do not have jobs. Reasons for the unemployment can be found in connection with all the other problems. Most reservations are far away from the cities where the jobs are. Many Native Americans do not get good jobs because of their outward appearance – some still like to wear long hair –, alcoholism, or their different lifestyle, for example their beliefs.

All these factors make it nearly impossible to break out of the vicious circle (= Teufelskreis), which means that most Native Americans also suffer from poor living conditions. Unemployment means lack of money. Lack of money results in a bad diet and cheap houses. If you look at the reservations you will find that most homes of Native Americans are corrugated-iron huts (= Wellblechhütte).

All in all, one should really ask oneself how human beings could ever bring other humans into such a situation. But the answer is easy: for the early settlers, Native Americans were humans of a lower class, more like animals really. We should learn from history and treat everyone the way we want to be treated ourselves.

4 Texte schreiben

Exercise 4 — Seite 92
1. In fact, indeed
2. What is more, they often have problems with alcohol.
3. On the one hand these problems date back to the time of the early European settlers; on the other hand they really need to do something themselves to improve their situation.
4. Compared with / In comparison with the situation of other minorities in the USA, Native Americans are, with regard to / with reference to working conditions, still underprivileged.
5. Nevertheless / Nonetheless, some Native Americans are very successful in their jobs.
6. Thus / Consequently / As a result / Accordingly / Therefore more and more Native Americans try to follow these examples.
7. Although many Americans still do not understand Native American culture, some Native Americans earn their living with tourism.
8. Furthermore, / Moreover, / Besides, the selling of Native American jewellery has turned out to be a real money-spinner in recent years.

4.2 Eine Reisebroschüre erstellen

Exercise 1 — Seite 93
Lösungsvorschlag:
When you are in Utah, you shouldn't miss Bryce Canyon National Park. Bryce Canyon fascinates the visitor with its sandstone rock formations, which glimmer in many different colors depending on the incidence of light.

Origin
Bryce Canyon is not actually a real canyon. It is part of the so called Pink Cliffs. Uncountable stone pillars, arches and rock pinnacles were carved out of the Paunsaugunt Plateau by rain, wind, ice and snow over millions of years.
About 60 million years ago the sea covered the southwest of Utah. On its bed lime, sand and mud were deposited and under the weight of the water pressed to firm stone. About 13 million years ago a massive tectonic movement set in, putting the land into slant. The result was that the water ran off, leaving the rock to the erosion of wind, ice and rain.

History of the National Park
Bryce Canyon was declared a nature reserve in 1928. In former times the Paiute used to live amongst the rock formations. They called it "Unka-tim-pewa-wince-pock-ich", which means "red rocks like standing men in a valley" – a very appropriate name. The National Park got its name from the Mormon settler Ebenezer Bryce who fought for the protection of this monument of natural beauty.

Sights
Right at the entrance to Bryce Canyon National Park is the Visitor Center. There you can get information about the Park. The center also shows slide shows and changing exhibitions. Close to the Center you can enjoy an amazing first view over the rock formations from the first of eleven lookout points, "Fairyland View".
One of the best ways to explore this fascinating work of nature is by walking. A network of a little more than 100 km of well-developed hiking trails stretches throughout the Canyon. "Rainbow Point" is the highest lookout point, located 2776 m above sea level.
A must-do, certainly, is a visit to the so-called amphitheater of sandstone, which is well known as the most impressive spectacle within the National Park. The Navajo Loop Trail leads from "Sunrise Point" through the rock pinnacles of "Queen's Garden" and back again. With a length of approximately 2.5 km and little less than 100 m in height to climb, this trail can be taken even by less fit people.

Highlights
Another way to explore the beauty of Bryce Canyon is on horseback, or something you will surely never forget is a helicopter scenic flight above Bryce Canyon. These tours start at Ruby's Inn and cost about $55 per person. Do not forget to bring your camera!

Accommodation
Best Western Ruby's Inn is the biggest hotel at the park, located near the main park entrance. Spread over a wide area, the hotel contains several restaurants, a souvenir shop and a western style village with jail and saloon. In the summer rodeos are offered, and of course the hotel has its

own swimming pool and campground. Contact: Best Western Ruby's Inn, Utah Hwy 63, Bryce, UT 84764. Phone: 435/834-5341. Price category: middle.

Bryce Canyon Lodge is the only accommodation inside the National Park. The buildings, which are about 80 years old, are made of massive logs. The Lodge offers 114 en suite rooms and 40 log cabins. Especially in the peak season the accommodation is regularly overbooked, so we strongly advise you to make your reservation at least eight months in advance. Contact: Bryce Canyon Lodge. Phone: 435/834-5361. Price category: middle.

Pink Cliffs Bryce Village is a simple hostel, located about 5 km from the entrance to the National Park. The rooms do without luxury but offer clean and cosy accommodation for little money. Contact: Pink Cliffs Bryce Village. Phone: 435/834-5303. Price category: lower – middle

For camping holidays we can recommend **North Campground,** which is close to the Visitor Center, **Sunset Campground** (4 km away from the Visitor Center) as well as the big campground at Ruby's Inn. Those three campgrounds offer parking spaces for trailers and campers as well as plenty of places for tents of all sizes.

- Information **Bryce Canyon National Park**, UT 84717. Phone: 435/834-5322
- Entrance fee: seven day pass per car: $10, seven day pass for one person with bike: $3.

4.3 Briefe verfassen

Exercise 1   Seite 98
Lösungsvorschlag:
Dear Mr. and Mrs. Sanderman,

My name is ... and I am writing because I am the German student who is going to stay with you in October this year. I received your address from my English teacher, Mrs. Schulz.
First of all, I would like to thank you for your kind offer to let me stay with your family while I am in the USA. I am already excited about the trip because I have not been to the USA before. I am also looking forward to meeting you and to staying with your family for three weeks.

Let me introduce myself. I am ... years old. I live in ... I like playing the ... and spend a lot of my free time with ... Enclosed you will find a photograph of me and my dog Lucy.
Do you have any children? I have got ... brothers and ... sisters. My mother works as a ... and my father is a .... We also have some pets: our dog Lucy is a German shepherd. But we also have some ...
But let me come back to my stay at your home. As my teacher has informed me, the planned program includes attendance at the local school in the mornings and excursions in the afternoons. That means that I will only be at your house in the evenings and at the weekends. I hope that this will be all right for you. Of course, I would be happy to help in the house in any way I can.
There is one thing that I feel I should tell you in advance. Unfortunately I neither eat fish nor hot tomatoes. I'm afraid I am allergic to them. But apart from those two things I eat everything, and I am also open to trying new things.
Please accept my apologies for any possible language mistakes in this letter. I hope my English will improve during my stay in your country.
Please feel free to correct me at any time. It will be a good way for me to improve.
I am looking forward to hearing from you soon and meeting you in October.

Best regards,
name

Exercise 2   Seite 98
1. Thank you for your friendly letter.
2. We are also very excited about your stay because we have never had a German pupil in our house before.
3. Now that you have told us so many things about yourself we are sure that we will get on with each other well.
4. You seem to be a very nice person and we have many things in common.
5. Let us tell you some things about us.
6. Our family consists of five people: mother Caroline, father Dan, Grandpa Jimmy, son Danny and daughter Jules.

4 Texte schreiben

7. Of course you can call all of us by our first names, as is usual in this country.
8. Oh, and we've got a dog, too; he's a Yorkshire terrier and his name is Brutus.
9. Danny is nearly fifteen years old, so you can go to school with him.
10. It is funny, but you have nearly the same hobbies, so I guess you will be good friends in no time.
11. Please write back as soon as possible and Danny will answer the next e-mail, so that you can get to know him better.
12. We are looking forward to meeting you soon.

Yours,
Caroline, Dan, Jimmy, Danny and Jules.

Exercise 3 Seite 99
Dear Mr Beckman,
Thank you for choosing Europe-America Student Exchange for your trip to the USA. Enclosed please find the tickets for your flight.
... our office at your convenience.
I would be happy to help in any way I can.

(Yours) sincerely, .../(Yours) truly, .../(Yours) faithfully, ...

4.4 Geschichten zu Bildern schreiben

Exercise 1 Seite 103
Lösungsvorschlag:
Dear Mum and Dad,

Greetings from Scotland. You know that at first I was not very happy about having to spend my holidays with Aunt Mary and Uncle Andy in this boring old castle. Especially since the weather is dreadful in Scotland at this time of year. So you can imagine that my mood was not very good when I arrived. Aunt Mary and Uncle Andy are very nice, that was a real surprise to me. Uncle Andy told me the story of the Spanish ghost one evening. Do you know the story?
Uncle Andy says that this Spanish tourist had visited the castle just before the First World War. Accidentally he had been locked in when the castle was closed for visitors in the evening. He had tried to get out, but the gates are made of iron and there is no escape without a key. He was rescued the next day. But Carlos, that's his name, liked the castle so much that when he was killed in World War One his ghost returned to the peace and quiet of this old castle.
I'm too old to believe in ghosts, so I nearly forgot about the whole story ... until yesterday.
It was another foggy day and Aunt Mary and Uncle Andy had to go to a birthday party. I didn't want to go with them, so they left me plenty of food and some DVDs, because they wanted to stay away the whole night.
In the early evening I decided to go for a walk before the sun went down. I have to admit that I even enjoy the quiet of the surroundings now. The fog makes the place look really mysterious and it's easy to imagine what it must have been like to live here at the time of the Scottish clans.
I had nearly reached the castle on my way back when I suddenly noticed that I had forgotten to take my keys. I had closed the big, wooden door and heavy iron gate of the castle when I left, as Aunt Mary had told me. But without my keys, I knew there was no way of opening them again.
Just the thought of a cold night outside the castle made me shiver. Even though there was no wind, I could feel it. There was a cold breeze in my face. Don't laugh at me, I swear I could feel it. I thought I was going mad when I suddenly heard a strange sound. It was as if the non-existent wind was saying "The gate, the gate ...".
And guess what I saw when I ran towards the gate? I was sure I had closed it, but when I looked at it, it swung open, just like in a storm.
I still don't understand what happened, but maybe there is a ghost after all?
I'll try to find out more and tell you about it in my next letter.
Love,
Kalli

Exercise 4 Seite 104
Lösungsvorschlag:
Tim was cycling as fast as he could along the road when he was overtaken by a car. The car driver, who wanted to turn left, did not see that Tim was

Texte schreiben 4

going straight on, and Tim did not notice the flashing indicators of the car. The driver turned, and Tim crashed straight into the car. The front wheel of his bike was smashed and he went flying over the top of the car and landed in the road. Fortunately he was wearing a helmet, so he only hurt his knee and elbow. An ambulance was called and his knee was bandaged up before they moved him from the road.
If you ask whose fault it was, I think it was more the fault of the car driver, because Tim was riding straight on so had right of way (= Vorfahrt). But it shows that kids on bikes should always keep their eyes open for what car drivers are going to do.

4.5 Zeitungsartikel schreiben

Exercise 1 Seite 107
headline: uses simple present because it is in the headline and the action is stressed, not its duration
l. 2: swapped: simple past to highlight the action
l. 4: had swapped: because the 'German guy's' action was clearly in a previous time frame
l. 7: had started: because the start of the autograph action is seen as being in an earlier time frame than the conclusion
l. 12–13: had a picture ... taken: somebody else took the picture („er ließ sich fotografieren")
l. 15: was hoping: past progressive because the focus is on the duration of the action
l. 16: was swapped: simple past passive because a particular action of the past is described and it does not matter who performed it
l. 29: think, see: simple present because (verbs of) knowing, feeling, perception cannot be viewed as ongoing activities
l. 31: after he had published: the publishing is the cause of people being able to follow his activities

Exercise 2 Seite 108
Who?   Ben Rosenbaum, 15
What? swapped his own autograph card for a car on the Internet
When? currently, recently
Where? San Diego, California

Why?   because he wanted to have a car and his grandfather gave him the idea by telling him about a German man who had done the same
How?   with the help of the Internet and the postal service

Exercise 3 Seite 109
Lösungsvorschlag:
Schlüsselwörter und -begriffe:
Tammy D., terrible argument with parents, run away, felt regret, wanted to come back, but was too afraid, sudden onset of winter, almost died in the cold, luckily the police found Tammy, she was still alive

Test

Exercise 1 Seite 110
1. D	6. T	11. C	16. G
2. L	7. N	12. S	17. P
3. B	8. J	13. O	18. E
4. K	9. Q	14. A	19. R
5. F	10. H	15. M	20. I

Exercise 2 Seite 110
1. Bitte entschuldigen Sie, dass ich so spät antworte.
2. Ich würde mich freuen, Ihnen irgendwie helfen zu können.
3. Ich stehe Ihnen für ein Gespräch zur Verfügung, wann immer es Ihnen passt.
4. Ich schreibe Ihnen in Bezug auf Ihr Jobangebot aus der Sonntagszeitung.
5. Bitte zögern Sie nicht mich zu kontaktieren, wenn Sie irgendwelche Fragen haben.
6. Vielen Dank für Ihre Zeit und Mühe.
7. Anbei finden Sie mein Foto und meine Adresse.
8. Ich würde mich über eine Antwort sehr freuen.
9. Ich möchte Ihnen für Ihre umgehende Antwort danken.
10. Könnten Sie mir bitte weitere Informationen zu der Arbeit geben?

Exercise 3   Seite 111

Lösungsvorschlag:
Dear Mother and Father,

I hope you are well. I have safely arrived in America now. The boat trip was terrible. We were on the ship for nearly three weeks. There were so many people there and not all of them survived. The smell was unbearable after a couple of days. When we arrived in New York I could see the Statue of Liberty. It is so big. It really gave me hope for the future. All the time on the ship I was worried about what lay before me. When I talked to other women on the journey, I found that I was lucky that I had a job waiting for me. But what would I do if the Stanfords were not satisfied with my work?

My biggest fear was that I wouldn't pass the medical examination. We all had to wait in a big hall. Then they examined every part of our bodies. I will never forget the cries of those who were sent back to Europe. All their dreams and hopes died in that hall. But I was lucky. The doctor said I was healthy and strong, so I was allowed to take the ferry from Ellis Island to New York.

New York is such a big city. There are thousands of people in the streets. It was hard to find my way to Brooklyn. Luckily I just had one suitcase to carry, but I spent most of my money just to reach the house of my employers.

The house where I now live is very big and beautiful. Mrs Stanford has got nice porcelain and wears expensive clothes. She treats me very kindly. She immigrated herself a couple of years ago, so she says she can imagine how I feel. Her four children are very well-behaved. They are all boys, just like my brothers at home. I guess I will get on well with the family.

I have already met other nannies in the playground, so hopefully I will have some friends in this unfamiliar country soon. My English is also getting better every day. Sometimes I have to ask, because I do not understand everything, but I am learning more and more words every day.

Please hug my brothers and sisters for me. I miss you all terribly and I hope that we will see each other again one day. Please take care of yourselves.

Lots of love,
Martha

© Cornelsen Scriptor

Bibliographisches Institut GmbH, Dudenstraße 6, 68167 Mannheim
ISBN 978-3-411-87079-0

Inhaltsverzeichnis

	Einführung	5

1	Kreatives Gestalten und Behinderung	7
1.1	Ästhetische Erziehung	10
1.2	Ästhetische Prozesse in Einrichtungen der Behindertenhilfe	12

2	Malerei	15
2.1	Theoretische Zusammenhänge	16
2.1.1	Grundlagen der Farbwahrnehmung	16
2.1.2	Psychologie der Farbe	17
2.1.3	Ordnungssystem der Farbe	19
2.1.4	Materialien und Werkzeuge	21
2.1.5	Organisation rund um das Gestalten mit Farbe	27
2.2	Praktische Umsetzung	29
2.2.1	Lockerungstechniken	29
2.2.2	Aleatorische Technicken	32
2.2.3	Farbexperimente	41
2.2.4	Gestalten mit Malkreiden	47
2.2.5	Malen als therapeutisches Mittel	50

3	Grafik	55
3.1	Zeichnung	56
3.2	Druckgrafik	59
3.2.1	Theoretische Zusammenhänge	59
3.2.2	Praktische Umsetzung	62

4	Gestalten mit Papier	71
4.1	Theoretische Zusammenhänge	72
4.2	Praktische Umsetzung	76

Inhaltsverzeichnis

5	Dreidimensionales Gestalten	83
5.1	Werkstoff Ton	85
5.1.1	Theoretische Zusammenhänge	86
5.1.2	Praktische Umsetzung	88
5.2	Werkstoff Pappmaschee	93
5.2.1	Theoretische Zusammenhänge	94
5.2.2	Praktische Umsetzung	95
5.3	Werkstoff Gips	100
5.3.1	Theoretische Zusammenhänge	100
5.3.2	Praktische Umsetzung	102
5.4	Werkstoff Holz	106
5.4.1	Theoretische Zusammenhänge	106
5.4.2	Praktische Umsetzung	110
5.5	Werkstoff Stein	112
5.5.1	Theoretische Zusammenhänge	113
5.5.2	Praktische Umsetzung	115
5.6	Werkstoff Metall	117
5.6.1	Material	117
5.6.2	Praktische Umsetzung	117
5.7	Objektkunst	118
5.7.1	Materialien und Werkzeuge	118
5.7.2	Praktische Umsetzung	119

Literaturverzeichnis	126
Bildquellenverzeichnis	128
Stichwortverzeichnis	129

Einführung

Das vorliegende Buch orientiert sich am Lehrplan für das Fach Werken/Gestalten an der Fachschule für Heilerziehungspflege bzw. Heilpädagogik. Damit wendet es sich als Handbuch für die Gestaltung des Unterrichts und gleichzeitig als Arbeitsbuch für das selbstständige Tun primär an Lehrende und Lernende an diesen Fachschulen. Mit seinen zahlreichen Anregungen kann es aber gleichzeitig ein Wegweiser sein für all jene, die Menschen mit Behinderung auf ihrem Lebensweg begleiten und sie zu eigenständigem schöpferischen Handeln ermuntern wollen.

Der immer wieder verwendete Begriff „Kunst" steht für die elementare gestalterische Aktivität eines jeden Menschen – ob mit oder ohne Behinderung. Es soll deutlich werden, dass jenseits der Reduzierung auf sogenannte „hohe Kunst" schöpferisches Gestalten mit künstlerischen Materialien stattfindet, welches als künstlerische Betätigungsform zu verstehen ist. Die Entfaltung kreativer Möglichkeiten, seien sie noch so gering, steht im Vordergrund, sodass bei allen pädagogischen Prozessen schöpferisches Handeln als subjektorientierte Aktivität konzipiert werden muss.

Im ersten Kapitel wird aufgezeigt, welche außerordentliche Bedeutung kreatives Gestalten mit künstlerischen Materialien für Menschen mit Behinderung besitzt. Die folgenden Kapitel sind den einzelnen Gestaltungsbereichen zugeordnet. Sie sind in sich abgeschlossen und können auch unabhängig voneinander verwendet werden. Die einzelnen Kapitel sind so aufgebaut, dass im Theorieteil zunächst grundlegende Informationen zu den einzelnen Gestaltungsbereichen zusammengetragen sind. Im Praxisteil werden zahlreiche Handlungsansätze vorgestellt, die schließlich durch Beispiele aus der Praxis transparent gemacht werden. Sinnvolle Fragestellungen und weiterführende Aufgaben ergänzen die einzelnen Abschnitte.

Das Buch basiert auf praktischen Erfahrungen in Schule und Einrichtungen. Es erhebt keinen Anspruch auf Vollständigkeit und kann gerne durch weitere Anregungen ergänzt werden.